The New Agenda for Higher Education

Choices Universities Can Make to Ensure a Brighter Future

K. Edward Renner

Detselig Enterprises Ltd.

Calgary, Alberta, Canada

© 1995 K. Edward Renner

Canadian Cataloguing in Publication Data

Renner, K. Edward (Kenneth Edward), 1936-
   The new agenda for higher education

   Includes bibliographical references and index.
   ISBN 1-55059-113-4

   1. Education, Higher—Aims and objectives. 2. Universities
and colleges—Curricula. 3. Universities and colleges—
Finance. I. Title.
LB2322.2.R46 1995   378'.001   C95-910550-6

Detselig Enterprises Ltd.
210-1220 Kensington Rd. N.W.
Calgary, Alberta, Canada
T2N 3P5

Cover Design by Bill Matheson

Detselig Enterprises Ltd. appreciates the financial assistance received for its
1995 publishing program from the Department of Canadian Heritage and the
Alberta Foundation for the Arts, a beneficiary of the Lottery Fund of the
Government of Alberta.

Printed in Canada   ISBN 1-55059-113-4   SAN 115-0324

Contents

COMMITTED TO THE DEVELOPMENT OF CULTURE AND THE ARTS

Preface

In 1980 I became a union negotiator for the Faculty Association for our collective agreement with Dalhousie University. At that time I became convinced that, unless decisive steps were taken, higher education was heading for what the Carnegie Council in *Three Thousand Futures* called the fears of some: men/women, white/black, students/faculty set against one another; problems of cost-containment; declining quality and loss of public confidence; retrenchment; internal conflict and loss of community.

I believe that the "good old days" of higher education, which started with the expansion of the 1960s, are over. Although most of us did not recognize it at the time, that period was *not* the start of something new, but rather it was the end of the Modern Era, which began with the transformations produced by the Industrial Revolution.

Now, 30 years later, is the start of something new. We now have an opportunity to shape the future during an historic time of transition. A new academic revolution is forming. Solutions to the growing list of issues have escaped us because our beliefs and assumptions about them are tied to the past and to the present, rather than to the future; they are in need of re-definition.

The process of re-definition is not new to the academic community; it is what we do best – at least when others rather than ourselves are the focus. Thomas Kuhn's description of scientific progress as being marked by periodic conceptual revolutions followed by refinement is a useful caricature for understanding the current state of higher education. It is in Kuhn's sense of a "paradigm shift" that I write about a new academic revolution.

We need new beliefs that will provide a set of concrete actions which can be undertaken, starting tomorrow morning at 7:30 A.M., to begin the process of the new "Academic Revolution" – of moving from the end of the Modern Era to what we are in the process of becoming. This requires meeting three challenges:

- The financial challenge is to create the *means* to be able to afford to replace the vicious negative cycle of retrenchment with a positive cycle of dynamism.

- The academic challenge is to have a vision of the *ends* that we wish to achieve to stop the destructive process of budget wars and to restore a sense of interdependency and community to the campus.

- The management challenge is to create a *process* through which the new academic revolution can take place.

In addition, we need problem solving which is both feasible and acceptable. This requires that the substantive issues of higher education and the process of change be treated as simultaneous – and not as successive or independent – conceptual tasks. There is no point in any individual figuring out a substantive solution and then in trying to convince all who are concerned that they are correct. There are many "correct" solutions. The separation of substance and process is one of the causes of current conflicts.

I believe that the 1990s are an exciting time to be alive; that tremendous energy and vitality is waiting to be claimed if we, who care deeply about higher education, can join in the process of the creation and the definition of a New Era.

My monograph clearly reflects a singular perspective of higher education: from someone who has spent 30 years as a university professor and who is deeply troubled by the way higher education appears to be drifting through – rather than participating in – the larger political, social and economic context. When I speak of "us" and "we," I am referring to those within higher education, like myself, for whom life has been directed at living out the varied roles and functions of higher education as a partial definition, as well as an extension, of ourselves.

I question many of the fundamental beliefs and values on which our colleges and universities are now proceeding. I hope that even the reader who disagrees with my assumptions and conclusions will give the ideas serious thought, and will seek to publicly challenge them to widen the current debate over the roles and functions of higher education. The issues and the choices before us are too important for anything less. This monograph is about many of the major current issues of higher education, including:

- cost-containment
- incoherence in the curriculum
- diversity
- retrenchment
- loss of community
- the renewal of the faculty
- new forms of scholarship
- teaching and learning
- accountability
- a new clientèle of learners

As a result of my convictions, I spent the last decade writing a series of research and conceptual papers about these issues and the need for change. This monograph is the cumulation of that work. I have now resigned my full-time position as university professor to pursue an career as an independent scholar and consultant in the area of higher education. I have retained an academic base as an Adjunct Research Professor at Carleton University to continue my research and association with students.

This book is for those who are directly or indirectly involved with higher education, including parents, students, faculty, administrators and government. It is also for all those who believe that higher education has gone astray and that a re-discovery of a sense of direction and purpose is essential.

If this monograph is successful in stimulating others to join in the adventure of a new academic revolution, I will have achieve my goal. Adventures are starting places with unknown outcomes, and this book, above all else, is an invitation to join in an adventure. If the reader has half as much fun reading the monograph as I did in writing it, we will both be more than satisfied.

Edward Renner
June, 1995
Ottawa, Ontario

Chapter 1
Introduction

Higher education is in the news. It has captured public interest. After a decade of internal debate over such issues as affirmative action, diversity, the curriculum, governance and retrenchment, these problems have now become public concerns and political issues.

The 1990s may well be the "Education Decade," extending from, at one end of the educational continuum, efforts to rescue our children from illiteracy to, at the other end, providing life-long learning to adults. Thus, any discussion of education, including higher education, must now recognize both the need for an internal self-examination of what is required, and for accountability to an external public for results. The problems of doing so fall largely into three categories: financial, academic and organizational.

Financial

Internally, universities are in difficult financial situations. Retrenchment became a buzz word on campuses in the 1980s, and with the economic recession of the early 1990s, it has resurfaced across North America with a renewed vigor. The financial pressure has divided academic units into conflicting camps of self-interest at a price of loss of community. The backlog of deferred maintenance is physical testimony to a slowly crumbling social institution. It has been a difficult time.

Externally, there has been growing competition for access to the public purse, resulting in a hard look at all the big spenders, which includes education. The public scrutiny of academic life, particularly from a business perspective where people are expendable but competitive survival is non-negotiable, has called in to question tenure and governance. With one-quarter of public taxes going to debt reduction, the urgency to end deficit financing, and a growing list of social demands, there is no reason to believe that higher education will ever again be out of close public review.

Academic

Internally, campus life has undergone significant changes in the last 30 years, altering the nature of institutions of higher education. The disappearance of liberal arts and women's colleges and the emergence of the multi-university are one illustration. Knowledge has become more inter-disciplinary. And, the rate of participation has dramatically increased, altering the variability of students in ability, gender, age and race. With a new clientèle has come a broader range of motivations and backgrounds of students and new concern over institutional roles and functions.

Externally, there are major social, economic and cultural transformations taking place. Descriptive phrases such as the Information Age, Global Community and New World Order capture the sense of a dynamic world-wide process of change. These external events have implications for all institutions, and in particular for higher education. Both critical thought and inquiry, and technological capacity are equally important to balance the humanities and science at a time of change in a way appropriate for the 21st century.

Organizational

Internally, there are leadership challenges arising from the diversity created by access, gender, age and race. The new and often competing demands of an increasingly complex social institution need to be managed. At the same time, the insular and isolated role of the past has given way to a growing expectation for higher education to be an active participant, an agent of change, in the larger context of what is called the "real" world.

Externally, higher education still enjoys public confidence in its value, if not in its current operational manifestations. But, there are divergent views on how education is to be structured and managed in the future. Governance is an issue precisely because the system too often seems irrelevant and unresponsive to external needs. The accountability movement and concern for cost-containment are two of the current intrusions in what institutions of higher education do, and how it is done.

Higher Education as a Social Issue

Higher education is no longer an island unto itself, to be left relatively alone to internally manage its own affairs. Colleges and universities are no longer *in locus parentis* to children nor are they immune from external intrusion. Promotion, tenure and student discipline are all open to legal review and the courts have over-turned internal decisions, requiring new internal ethics and procedures.

It is for reasons such as these that I have defined higher education as a social issue. When a topic becomes a concern to a significant number of people, external to those directly involved, the focus of attention enters the political and social realm, and, by definition, it becomes a social issue.

Solving Social Problems

Social problems require different types of solutions than technical problems. A group of civil and structural engineers may make a technical decision on the best spot for a bridge over a river based on the terrain. But, once the location of the bridge becomes a social or political concern, the problem takes on new dimensions. If the nesting patterns of Blue Herons are not to be disturbed, then the actual technical problem may be how to build the bridge at a place no expert would choose, or else to win the debate that nesting Blue Herons are expendable.

Such debates are not easy to win. There is some sense in which the welfare of animals at the city zoo has a better chance of competing for scarce resources than homeless men, as a budget controversy illustrated in the Spring of 1991 in New York City (*New York Times*, June 19, 1991).

It is not that higher education was never a social problem; clearly, to a degree, it has always been of public concern. However, now more than ever before, it is of concern to a larger and growing number of constituent groups, each with a social or political philosophy and corresponding agenda. In short, higher education, like the homeless, has become a social issue.

Thus, solutions are not just in the hands of higher education "engineers." While the philosophy of higher education is still a legitimate academic discipline, it is becoming increasingly peripheral to what higher eduction is about. Higher education must be conceptualized and approached in a political and social way, as well as from the technical perspective of higher education as expressed in graduate schools of higher education administration, institutes and centres for research in higher education, and in their various journals and professional associations.

Social problems and issues have a life and complexity of their own, and preeminence of thought and strategy must often be given to their non-technical aspects.

The Organization of the Monograph

Because this monograph is about higher education as a social problem, it brings together two very different discourses. On the one hand the book is about the issues of higher education, such as the curriculum, retrenchment and cost-containment, but on the other hand, it is also about how to solve social problems.

I have divided the material into five sections. Each section contains discussions of issues of higher education – the concepts and issues that are **internal** in the sense that educators discuss them with each other at educational conferences. And, in addition, each section contains discussions of the place of higher education in modern North American society – concepts and issues that are **external** in the sense that there is a clashing of controversial social and political influences, typical of social issues.

Section One: Context

Section One provides an interpretive review of higher education to set the tone for the rest of the book. The first chapter is a brief examination of how the present state of affairs came about. It is intended to give the reader who is not a specialist in higher education enough information to have a starting point.

The second chapter describes the perspective I will use to make value judgements and to evaluate and interpret facts. I do not argue extensively for the validity of my assumptions relative to other logical possibilities. I simply present them as information which is necessary in order to understand the material which follows. It will remain for other chapters to provide the detailed analysis required to critically evaluate these assumptions, and then to either accept or reject the position I am advancing.

If the reader can accept my assumptions, then the analysis of the problems and the proposed solutions will follow. If the assumptions seem too outrageous, then I invite the reader to temporarily suspend their own assumptions, to move into my frame of reference and to give me an opportunity to make my case.

The major point of Section One is that social problems are solved through the process of re-definition. Specifically, *it is the beliefs which people hold which lock them into inflexible dead ends and, alternatively, which can create new potential.* Changing beliefs is a social and psychological process, and it is in this sense that higher education as a social issue is only partly about education.

Section Two: Re-Defining Beliefs

Section Two examines existing and alternative beliefs. I call such beliefs "templates" because they are portable and relative – they may be carried from one situation to another and used in various combinations. Templates are "forceful" because once they are used they determine how events are seen, and in this way shape the perceived character of the event.

Beliefs are the basis of much of our stubbornness and of our creative capacity. The process of re-definition brings a new set of beliefs to bear on an old issue, but in a way which significantly alters how it is seen and the options which are available. Such a proposition, of course, implies that knowledge is socially constructed and that discovery is more a matter of our mind than of the "true" objective nature of the natural order. Whether this philosophy of knowledge is appropriate for all things is not of concern to me in this monograph; it is, I have found, an extremely useful approach to solving social problems, and it is particularly appropriate for the current issues of higher education. I claim no more.

In the four chapters of this section, I describe two dozen bi-polar dimensions. One end of various combinations of these dimensions can be used to describe and understand most of the current issues of higher education. However, shifting the perspective to an alternative contrasting belief will cast the issue into an entirely new light, re-defining it in a way which presents new alternatives and new options.

For example, as long as the problems of higher education are defined as external, general and geographic (national, state, provincial or regional) by those of us who are within higher education, we will be powerless to solve them. Instead, we will be dependent on others to rescue us, and, when they do not, we will grow angry at them, as we are now doing. In contrast, if we can re-define these problems as internal, specific and local we can create immediate opportunities for effective leadership and for solving our problems through self-directed actions. To fail to define our problems in ways that allows us to effectively engage the issues is to set ourselves up for continuing "us" versus "them" conflicts over our future.

It is here in Section Two that the assumptions described in Section One are important. The assumptions provide the overview, making it possible to identify the specific two-dozen beliefs which are necessary, out of all of the beliefs which are theoretically possible. With this set of beliefs in hand, it is possible to both understand higher education as a social issue, and begin at once to solve the resulting problems.

Section Three: Opportunities

The new beliefs lead to specific problem-solving approaches for responding to the financial, academic and organizational challenges listed at the start of this chapter. While no one would choose to face three such formidable issues at once, they may be viewed as constructive opportunities for developing problem-solving approaches which otherwise would not have been possible.

Challenges can be seen as threats for which defensive reactions to protect the status quo are necessary; but such reactions are seldom effective. This is especially true if the challenges arise from circumstances which have rendered obsolete the old ways. Under conditions of change, serious challenges are best treated as opportunities to develop proactive ways of responding.

Responding to challenges as opportunities is similar to an adventure into the unknown. True to an adventure, genuine problem solving is a process for creating and managing change; it is not a pre-determined *product* which divides people into conflicting camps based on those that will be better off and those that will be worse off. Rather, a problem-solving process moves beyond power struggles by actively engaging those who are affected to assume responsibility for finding solutions based on new ways of thinking.

Section Four: Change

Section Four provides a set of values necessary for turning challenges into opportunities. Achieving true change requires a higher order conceptual framework to provide an explicit understanding of the objectives and a set of operational constraints to insure that the process opens new opportunities by responding to the challenge.

Values and approaches for implementing them are debatable. The three chapters in this section – one on higher education, one on the social and psychological aspects of solving social problems, and one on management – provide the philosophy for getting on with the process of re-definition and of using problem-solving processes in a public, responsible and accountable way.

These chapters carry the weight of turning the previous material from an academic exercise into an actual demonstration project worthy of merit.

Section Five: Prospect

Section Five provides a glimpse of the total implications of the monograph. The result is an exciting new university in the forefront of a transitional period of human history.

Our colleges and universities have an opportunity to be the most exciting institutions in the nation with which to be associated. There is a place waiting to be claimed.

Joining an Adventure

Re-definitions require a playful state of mind. This book is about an adventure. The reader is, above all else, to have a good time. The starting point is to at least temporarily adopt the mind set that now is a new era of human history and that experimenting with new ways of thinking is a useful way to solve problems.

Section One
Context

This section contains two chapters. The first chapter places the specific internal issues of concern to higher education – such as retrenchment, diversity and loss of community – in their recent historical context. The second chapter then places higher education into the larger external context of history, economics, change theory and the applied realm of problem definition and problem solving.

At the present, three major challenges face higher education. There were clear warnings of them in 1980 as problems which, if not addressed, would become major challenges by the 1990s, as they have indeed become. The first of these was the limit on financial resources which would create a financial challenge over the *means*. The second was the implications of student, faculty and population demographics which would alter the nature of colleges and universities, resulting in an academic challenge over their *ends*. And the third was accountability for their effectiveness which would result in a management challenge over *process*. These issues are largely factual and historical.

However, the interpretation of these historical "facts" is a far different issue. Because there are many possible perspectives I will be explicit about the assumptions I will use to impose meaning and to propose solutions. I have identified four themes which will reappear throughout the text, providing the foundation on which the rest of the material depends. They are: First, that now is an epochal time in history; second, that these are the good times economically; third, that fundamental, not incremental, change is necessary; and fourth, that it is our beliefs that are both the source of the problems and the means for a solution.

Chapter 2
Not Without Warning

We have understood for some time the critical issues of higher education. In 1980, in the U.S., the Carnegie Council published *Three Thousand Futures: The Next Twenty Years for Higher Education*, and in Canada, the Association of Universities and Colleges of Canada published *Canadian Universities: 1980 and Beyond* (Leslie, 1980). Both of these books provided accurate projections of the 1980s, and we have every reason to believe that their view for the 1990s will be just as perceptive.

Anticipating the future of higher education is easier than most forms of future gazing. The traditional clients of higher education give a 20-year advance warning of their arrival, and the universities of the 1960s and 1970s were the primary producers of the research and critical thought, and the generation of people from which the trends of the present have been forged.

Finances

We have known since the early 1970s that roughly between the years 2000 to 2010 two-thirds of the faculty will reach the age of 65, and that in the 15 years prior to this period – 1985 through 2000 – they will reach the top of the salary scale. The rapidly escalating size of the salary budget will be well in excess of the inflation rate (Renner, 1986c). The inevitable result is severe retrenchment pressures with little academic or financial flexibility, the major effects of which are yet to be felt (Renner, 1987). A typical university faculty budget at constant dollars (which is a best case scenario because new money has not kept pace with real cost increases) will require a 15% reduction in the number of faculty by the year 2000 due simply to the age bulge moving up the salary scale without an even flow of retirements off the top and replacements at the lower salary levels. The exact percentage and time of impact will vary by institution and discipline depending on the local hiring pattern in the 1960s and the age distribution of the current faculty. For the next decade, there must be either significantly more money for salaries, from some place, or else fewer faculty. There is no other apparent choice.

Salary costs account for 95% (for disciplines with laboratory classes such as chemistry and theatre) to 99% of *departmental* budgets (Renner, 1988a). Higher education is labor intensive. The only place to reduce costs is through reductions to the faculty and academic services. Cost-containment and budget management will limit salary increases and put upward pressure on tuition, creating management/labor divisions, increasing work load, decreasing quality and dividing the university community into camps on the basis of economic self-interest. The foundation of the university will shift from academic to financial mechanisms as the driving force behind decisions, with budgets increasingly determining academics, rather than academic considerations determining budgets.

The Financial Challenge

We have been forewarned of these facts since 1980. The past decade has shown the predictions to be accurate as reflected by the title of the lead chapter "A House Divided" in the book *College* by Earnest Boyer (1987) of the Carnegie Foundation, and the loss of a sense of community found in a survey of US colleges and universities (Carnegie Foundation, 1990a). Another decade remains to play out these trends to their logical conclusion. The warning in 1980 was that cycles of retrenchment and cost-containment efforts would reduce the capacity to react, change and adapt, resulting in the need for further retrenchment: A vicious negative circle. The prophecy is fast becoming a reality.

The prescription by the Carnegie Council in 1980 to avoid this negative cycle was for "dynamism." Dynamism was not then, and is not now, a catchy word for begging the question, as it has been treated. Rather, it is a concept. It has the same foundation in reality as "retrenchment," but it is the reciprocal in terms of process. Over the past decade all available resources should have been directed into changes which would have anticipated the future, instilled change and allowed adaptations promoting the process of vitality: A dynamic positive circle. The financial challenge is to replace the vicious circle of retrenchment by creating the *means* to provide enough financial flexibility to create the positive *ends* of "dynamism." The difficulty of the task now – in contrast to 1985 – is compounded by having lost valuable time (one-half the critical period), good will (the house is divided) and resources (investment capital was used to support the status quo while the purchase of essential maintenance of buildings, books and teaching equipment was deferred).

Demographics

Over the past decade, the focus on demographics has been almost exclusively on the traditional college-age student and the "demographic depression" due to reach the bottom in the mid to late 1990s. However, faculty and population demographics also have important implications for higher education, but although equally well known, they have been given little attention until very recently.

Students

The decline in the numbers of traditional college-age students was the only warning which was heard and heeded. It was clear that the decline in the absolute numbers of 18-26 year olds need not result in a decrease in the total number of students if the loss could be off-set by a greater participation rate, or, alternatively, by tapping the new markets of adult and life-long learning.

These new markets were readily identifiable, and for the most part have been reached to the degree necessary to keep classrooms and dorms full, and indeed, bring tuition-paying students per square foot to the tolerable limit. Given our human nature, adaptation takes place and the threshold for over-crowding can be inched upward. And, through the psychological process of cognitive dissonance, some students can be induced to believe that their over-crowding is evidence that they are the lucky ones and should be thankful, meaning compliant.

In Canada, which has had a relatively low participation rate in comparison to the United States, the approach of least resistance has been to expand the traditional base, in particular to women. In both countries, the economic slow-down has helped this effort, as middle and upper socio-economic students have sought more and higher levels of credentials. To date, the financial necessity for over-flowing classrooms has not yet contributed, *proportionally*, to increased access for the poor and marginal – as will be discussed in detail in Chapter 11 (Renner, 1993).

Faculty

The age distribution of the faculty has more than just financial implications. In addition to being middle-aged, they are mostly a homogeneous group of white men who have been teaching for over two decades. No institution can go 20 – let alone 35 – years without significant renewal without losing vitality. Yet, this is the situation in higher education. Creative scholarship is perhaps more dependent on vitality through renewal than are most enterprises. The 1985 and 1989 Carnegie Foundation (1989) surveys found that many faculty are tired and without vision. Further, graduate programs have been curtailed and what was formerly a high prestige academic career no longer attracts our best minds; the supply line has been seriously interrupted (Altbach & Lewis, 1992).

Out-placements, voluntary separations and early retirements are common in business and industry to ensure vitality through continuous renewal. We know that to provide the disillusioned faculty with the financial support required for a graceful, voluntary exit, and to replace them with young faculty, would cost far less over the time period to their scheduled retirement than their salaries. The optimum time for starting this process was in 1985, spreading the coming problem due to many retirements and few available replacements over an extra 15 years. Graduate programs already could have been growth areas. Rather, higher education has waited. There is now less room for maneuvering, and an aging faculty, mostly male, who are willing and able to stay, at a high financial and academic cost. The shortage in the supply line will drive up salaries of the required young replacements as well.

Population

We have known ever since they were born that by the year 2000 the first of the baby boomers will reach the age of 55. From that time on, the proportion of working people in comparison to those who are dependent – the young and old – will steadily decline. Thus, the necessary future supply of students and trained workers can only be achieved through more adult learners and through increasing the participation rates of those – the poor and people of color – who were promised but did not achieve equality and inclusion in the 1960s. However, unlike then, a transformation of class and color will need to become a reality through the economic necessity of the relative shortage of workers in comparison to the large numbers who will be old (Renner, 1992).

The Academic Challenge

These known demographic facts have left higher education with the challenge of gaining the academic flexibility required for renewed vitality and for meeting new educational needs. These are the issues of creating the capacity for colleges and universities to become responsive to their clients of the future.

The New Students

As the numbers of traditional-aged students are increasingly offset by non-traditional students, the pressures will increase for higher education to adapt what they do in order to meet new and different student needs. We should expect growing tension over who should adjust. If higher education does not change, the mature and life-long learners may well take their business elsewhere, as indeed, the resurgence of community colleges suggests is happening. Half of all undergraduates are now adults (Chabotar & Honan, 1990), although the composition of the traditional university has changed only marginally.

Further, industry has recognized the growing need for trained workers, and that students are not coming from colleges and universities with the required skills. The training business gives to their employees may either continue to take the form of flex time and financial incentives for attaining additional post-secondary credits; or, it could well take the form of increased in-house training on the skills and knowledge most relevant to that business – be it computers or languages (Eurich, 1985; 1991). We can expect, however, that the emphasis will be on *training* more than *education*, a role for which current academics do not feel entirely comfortable. Faculty are already critical of their existing students for being too career-centred (Carnegie Foundation, 1989).

The Old Faculty

We have not yet seriously addressed the academic effects of the age bulge of the faculty. The numbers and composition of the current faculty are such that women and minorities cannot hope to make appreciable gains in this decade. Providing role models for the students who are to be the new generation of scholars has been over-taken by the need, even though the process has not yet started. To this culture gap we must add the generation gap and the communication distance becomes even greater.

The trends in the 1985 and 1989 National Survey of Faculty have been summarized by the Carnegie Foundation (1989) and the raw data reported in the *Chronicle of Higher Education* (Jacobson, 1985; Mooney, 1989). Interpretations have varied dependent upon whether the focus is on the faculty who are happy or unhappy. It is, of course, a relative judgement how many negative attitudes reflect a "stable and stagnate" faculty (Watkins, 1986). The absolute judgement aside, significant numbers among the faculty are hankering after the past for a return to a good "old" liberal education. They want students to be less career-oriented and better prepared, and as many (44%) find their work a source of considerable personal strain as those who do not (45%). At least one in five wants out of his or her job as a professor, maybe more.

In recent history, renewal through growth has been the mechanism for vitality; colleges and universities have not had renewal for some time, nor is there an immediate prospect of any (Bowen & Schuster, 1986). Yet, at an epochal time, vitality is essential, even more so now than in the 1960s when expansion and extension of the nationalism articulated by John Kennedy – not change – was the inspiration.

Difficult Adjustments

F Although increasing the numbers of students has been relatively easy, living with the consequences has not, and will become less so in the future. Colleges and universities have already engaged in "registration wars" as declining numbers of potential students and a heavy reliance on tuition for income has forced more aggressive recruiting practices (Wilson, 1990a, 1990b; Collison, 1992). The trend toward grade inflation and stepped up efforts at better retention through remedial intervention have all contributed to maintaining numbers, but with the side effect of growing criticism by the faculty of under-prepared students who do not have the motivation to learn for the sake of learning.

Further, the decline in the absolute number of traditional-aged students in the population is only partially completed; the biggest impact of the demographic depression remains to come (Carnegie Council, 1980; Chabotar & Honan, 1990). Off-setting the initial decline has produced major stress in academia, but it is merely the precursor to things to come. The opportunity to develop proactive strategies is over. The adaptations necessary to accommodate increased numbers and a wider range of abilities and motivations should have been completed, but faculty have resisted changing their expectations or their teaching methods. Divisions of instructional resources, which have been set up on many campuses to help professors adapt to the needs of their new customers, have not had their doors broken down by faculty asking for help, nor has teaching support fared well in a period of restraint. Rather, even the simplest of tools – such as chalk – are often missing, along with equipment, adequate computers and audio-visual aids. Teaching and learning effectiveness is close to out of control; so much so that teaching and learning has had to be "re-discovered" as a campus issue.

Accountability

There are two major issues: How well is higher education doing? And, are the costs within tolerable limits?

Teaching and Learning

We have known for many years about teaching and learning styles. In the language of current reform we have "collaborative learning" and "service learning" as models, and there are many examples of the popularity of classes which successfully bridge disciplines by combining academics with life (in particular on the environment and world political order). These manifestations all give testimony to the fact that education understands the model, and has since at least as long as Illach's *Deschooling of Society* (1971), through to modern experiential education. The philosophy and theory has been clearly defined.

Higher education – for a variety of reasons – has chosen against clear warnings to maintain a university incentive system which rewards research and which separates learning from living at the very time when the rate of change makes it imperative to reduce such temporal distances. Academics have been the principal financial beneficiaries of such distancing mechanisms as certification, professionalization and credentialization. "It's time for results" was the title of the report of the Association of Governors (Alexander, 1986) which put political clout behind mandated accountability. And Lamar Alexander, in his tenure as the Secretary of Education, attempted to carry through on this agenda.

The assessment movement which has developed in response to these external demands has brought the language of higher education to bear on accountability. The new robes look good; the external pressure has been co-opted, for now, and colleges and universities have bought precious time. But, results will be required. However, whether fundamental structural change is underway is debatable. There is the possibility that higher education is marking time by riding a reform movement to encourage attention to quality when radical change is the challenge – change which goes beyond ensuring an adequate supply of chalk.

Cost-Containment

Only the extraordinary high regard that American society has for higher education can account for the fact that through a difficult economic decade, higher education has been able to raise its tuition costs faster than inflation without massive public indignation. Yet, despite the increases, colleges and universities have fallen further behind; the piper of deferred maintenance is yet to be paid, estimated to now be over $70 billion (Grassmuck, 1990b), up from $20 billion two years before (Fuchsberg, 1988). The bubble will burst. A decade of grace has been wasted, to now be faced with the necessity of real cost-containment. But, most of the flexibility that was available is gone – such as using temporary faculty when permanent faculty have died or resigned – and few untouched resources remain.

The response of importing business management techniques has been poorly received, contributing to rather than reducing traditional labor/management divisions. "Growth by substitution" requires vertical cuts – which are politically divisive and create the lifeboat mentality that undermines the needed cooperation. The retrenchment solutions of horizontal cuts and hiring freezes used to date have reduced internal coherence through change dictated by chance and circumstance, further weakening the product, undermining public confidence and hastening the day of reckoning.

The snowball is rolling and gaining mass, with force and direction of its own. There is an accountability crisis in higher education. The newest discovery – Total Quality Management (TQM) – is the first sign that higher education may be willing to look at is own internal structure and procedures as the systemic source of many of the problems and as the potential for solutions.

The Management Challenge

The academic challenge of teaching and learning requires, if not more, at least different academic services, more not less faculty, smaller not larger classes, and new interactive not traditional teaching methods. If achievement of these academic ends are directly linked to increased financial flexibility, each requiring the other as a precondition, then there is indeed a management problem.

However, even if more financial resources were to be made available, dynamism is not assured. The academic decision-making process is designed for **entrenchment** of individualism and independent scholarship. The academy is not easily tampered with externally by others who may have a different agenda from the freedom to be an academic that colleges and universities have sought to protect. While the mechanisms which have insulated faculty from external influence have served them well in the past, it is not now other people, but rather – paradoxically – those protective structures against intrusive change that stand in the way of achieving new internal goals and objectives. Higher education never anticipated that the fundamental concept of academic freedom could be its own enemy.

It is in this sense that I use the term of an "academic revolution," because it is the conception higher education has of itself, as well as those beliefs within higher education that are held about others and about the external context, which must be included in the discourse.

Thus, the management challenge has two faces. First, to manage change in the face of what appears to be a dilemma of first needing either academic or financial flexibility to achieve the other. And second, to be an agent of change in an academic revolution which threatens the status quo and therefore the conferred source of authority required for internal academic leadership.

Heeding the Warning

All three of these challenges were foreshadowed in great detail. The only surprise, perhaps, was how superficially easy the warning of the demographic depression was to heed, at least in a numerical sense. However, it is not yet clear that higher education is prepared to deal with the academic consequences of this economic action. There is no reason to believe that the other warnings – now manifest as the current crisis in higher education – would have been, or still are, any more difficult, had they been engaged with the same determination as was used to maintain enrollment levels. The problems are not particularly complicated or difficult as problems go; however, the social and psychological process of choosing to engage them are.

At the end of World War II higher education had a clear role, which it has now carried out to its logical conclusion. But, it no longer has within it such a vision. No longer is higher education committed, as it was then, to creating the future, but is now reacting to it as if it were a hostile force, rather than an opportunity for imagination and a source of anticipation – it has lost its sense of direction and purpose. This has been the decade of retrenchment, and the malaise should be expected.

If higher education is to regain a vision for the future, then it must ask why it did not heed so clear a warning. What was the thinking that could have allowed the academy to fall so far behind? What should we believe about higher education instead?

Chapter 3
Assumptions

How could higher education have fallen so far behind? How could it have happened so fast? The extent of the problems within a single generation of faculty underscores the need for examining our beliefs about history, economics, change and problem solving.

An Epochal Period

"It was the best of times, it was the worst of times, it was the age of wisdom, ✦ it was the age of foolishness, it was the epoch of belief, it was the epoch of incredulity." With those words, in *A Tale of Two Cities*, Dickens captured the contradictions of the industrial and political revolution that started the Modern Era. We have now reached the end of that era, and once again, "we have everything before us, we have nothing before us."

Revolutionary times hold new promises, but without certainty of what the ✦ outcome will be; they demand taking risks, but without providing security. Such times are difficult. People and institutions need certainty of purpose and security of self to openly risk boldness, yet when boldness is required in epic proportions, both are absent.

In higher education, two revolutionary processes are simultaneously under way; one is internal and the other is external. The internal revolution concerns the re-definition of research, teaching and scholarship. The professorate has the problem of reaching non-traditional age-gender-race students in the face of a decade of documentation of growing cultural, mathematical and scientific illiteracy, perhaps beginning with a *Nation at Risk* (National Commission, 1983), but certainly not ending with Bloom (1987) and Hirsch (1987).

The external revolution concerns the end of the Modern Era and the beginning of what some have called the "Age of Knowledge." By whatever name, it is similar in scope to the industrial and political revolution which went before. The academy, rightly, is expected to be on the cutting edge of critical thought required for this social transformation. This is our *raison d'être*. What an exciting place the university should be!

Yet, the academy has left the battle of human existence to be preoccupied with family troubles amidst external criticisms for failing to teach. Internally, the economic consequences of the external revolution – called retrenchment, a defensive gesture – has diminished the certainty of purpose and the security of the status quo and it has been experienced as a threat. This struggle by colleges and universities to protect their own survival, as they traditionally know and value it, has prohibited them individually and collectively, at least for the moment, from getting on with their own internal revolution. However, until they do, they will remain on the sidelines of an epoch of social change.

Thus, another paradox. The stability necessary for meeting either the internal challenges (i.e., external stability) or the external challenges (i.e., internal stability) are both absent. Yet, the solution to one is a prerequisite for the other. The dilemma is captured by the conflicting leadership role of needing to be both, at one and the same time, a manager of change and an agent of change.

The End of the Modern Era

The last show of academic boldness, in the 1960s, was based on the economic security of growth and the sense of certainty in the virtue of the joint quests to meet the challenges of Sputnik and of greater equality and social justice through wider access to education. New money was provided for a new generation of scholars to let all people share in the fulfillment of the dreams of the Modern Democratic State and Industrial Era.

All that remains is the disillusionment of those dreams; there was no pot of gold for everyone at the end of that rainbow. The rap music of Fight the Power chronicles the failure of the industrial and political revolution to achieve for Blacks, among others, the promises that had marked the beginning of the Modern Era. But, it is over. The 1960s were the last dying gasps of the efforts of the terminal generation of this era to fulfil those promises. What is to be achieved by the democratic-industrial era has been achieved. The final account-ing of the shortfall of broken promises is a deficit to be reckoned with in a new way in a new time. It should not be surprising that what *Time* (July 16, 1990) called the "twenty-something generation" has no clear profile. The past is clearly over, and the future has no clarity.

The New Academic Revolution

The internal adjustments required by colleges and universities to meet the external revolution requires leadership which can internally manage change. Undoubtedly, this is one of the contributing factors to the growing interest in the importation of business management techniques to the university. However, the external context simply does not provide, as it did in the 1960s, the support – certainty of purpose and economic security – necessary to foster basic internal change within academia.

Meeting the challenges of accountability, cultural diversity, adult learning and the national goal of technological competitiveness will create immense internal instability. The new academic revolution requires internal leadership to assume ownership of these challenges by becoming agents of fundamental change. Revolutions, by definition, overturn existing power and authority which illegitimately protect the privileges of the past. But rarely, if ever, will existing authority be used to destroy the basis of its own legitimacy.

Now are the Good Times

It is also hard for higher education to accept the economic view that now are the good times when the *Chronicle* reports that for the 1990-91 academic year the growth rate for state spending on higher education was at a 30-year low (Jaschik, 1990), followed by mid-term budget reduction in 30 states (Cage, 1991), all leading toward a two-year decline in state support (Jaschik, 1992). And for 1993, the annual survey of state budgets by the *Chronicle* showed no relief in sight either for the current year or for the rest of the decade (Lively & Mercer, 1993). But, population demographics and stronger competing demands for public support should make clear that these are the good times.

Population Demographics

The term "demographic depression" was a concept which created a myopic focus of attention – of a panoramic historical episode – on that period when the supply of college-age students would dramatically decline following the last of the baby boomers. Of far greater importance is the impact of this large group at other moments in time. In 1965 at the end of the baby boom, 70% of the US population was classified by the Bureau of Census as a dependent – under 15 or over 65 years of age. By 1985, the last of the baby boomers had turned 25 and entered the work force. The first of them, however, will not reach age 55, the beginning of early retirement, until the year 2000. Combined with the fallen birth rate, which is below replacement levels, and the relatively small number of people who are now old because of the effects of the depression and World War II, the United States has the smallest proportion of dependents (a combination of the young and old) and the largest proportion of people in the work force in its history. The tax base between the years 1985 and 2000 is as good as it is ever going to be. The opportunity to change ourselves and to claim the future is during this 15-year period.

It is true that there will be a small upswing in the numbers of traditional-age students after the turn of the century, but, just as adult learners off-set the decline during the late 1980s, and may or may not do so in the mid-1990s, their smaller numbers after the year 2000 may not be compensated for by the little boom. The economic benefits of broad population demographics are now on the side of colleges and universities. By the year 2025 the number of dependent people in the population will return to its 1965 level (70%) when the baby boomers were all children, except now they will be grandparents.

Competing Demands

The growing demands for public money from energy, debt servicing, the environment, health care and dislocations from competing in a world economy have not yet been fully felt. Higher education will get its share of public funds, but no more. In economic terms, these are the good times. It is time to get on with the internal revolution rather than waiting for better times.

There is no longer academic or financial flexibility, and this is widely recognized. The attacks on the tenure system in books such as *Prof-Scam* (Sykes, 1989) in the United States and *The Great Brain Robbery* (Bercuson, Bothwell & Granatstein, 1984) in Canada go to the heart of the matter. People outside academia no longer believe tenure is needed to protect academic freedom; they believe those safeguards now exist in our political system and that tenure has become an outdated concept protecting, instead, the vested economic interest of professors, who do not seem to be listening to reasonable requests to be more accountable.

In the face of competing demands (from homeless men to the shift from the cold war toys of star wars, to the next military phase of regional "pacification" of the ghettos of the world, and perhaps urban areas at home) the public purse will not pay for both the status quo, which will exceed inflation increases in every year of this decade, *and* provide additional money for all of the new roles and functions that are so clearly needed. Higher education has held out for greater public funding to the point where it now faces the ultimatum that enough is enough.

Change or Be Changed

There are two contexts, the internal and the external, which are out of synchronization. As an example, higher education is expected to participate in a period of rapid social change in the external world. However, our colleges and universities are turned inward, preoccupied by family troubles. As a result, cost-containment, increases in tuition, a disjointed curriculum and the quality of teaching and learning are all under critical examination.

The external perception is that tenure and academic freedom have outlived their usefulness in modern democracy, and that they are being used to protect the status quo and to resist necessary and appropriate internal change. The internal experience is of a state of siege, of being caught in the impossible dilemma of being expected to deliver new services, but without having the means to do so. Two perceptions, two realities and no apparent way out.

No one else is going to rescue higher education. The warnings are loud and clear, for higher education either has to change what is done and how it is done, or be changed. Universities are expected to meet the new roles and responsibilities of life-long learning, national competitiveness, diversity and quality. These are reasonable expectations.

However, as long as there are limited resources and no means for increased academic and financial flexibility, all that remains is an apparent dilemma: the choice of either internally-directed retrenchment, with an array of negative alternatives that will continue to divide the university community into conflicting camps of self-protection and self-justification, or of doing nothing and inviting imposed solutions for accountability which will subject the curriculum, faculty appointments and tenure, and university management to external interference. Thus, the dilemma: a choice between two equally unacceptable courses of action.

Dilemma and Re-definition

Such dilemmas are difficult to solve because of the way the issues are defined. Whenever there appears to be only two alternatives, both unacceptable to one party or the other, the tendency is to struggle over whose definition shall prevail. The conclusion I reach is that, more often, the only satisfactory resolution is through re-definition, of recasting the problem in a way which no longer requires a one-sided solution.

The dilemmas of higher education are products of our own minds. Whenever people feel like they have a choice between being shot or hanged, it is time to question the framework which presents the choice, not to debate the relative merits of the unacceptable. The escape is not to "discover" the greater truth between the existing alternatives, but to re-define the issues in ways which present new alternatives which are both feasible and acceptable.

Examining assumptions should always be the first order of business whenever daily activities are dominated by reacting to the unwanted, unplanned and unexpected. Like science, anticipated (i.e., predicted) results only confirm what we already believed and allow us to move forward with confidence. Negative results, however, are the basis of progress. The unexpected is seldom bad luck, but rather an invitation to invent new concepts and to move forward with a sense of experimentation and adventure. The successful end of the exercise is new concepts which eliminate surprise and restore routine and order to forthcoming events which are once again predictable, and therefore ones for which we can be well prepared.

This view of the important role of our assumptions is not a rose-colored prescription for spinning straw into gold. It is hard and difficult work. Troubled times have come to higher education and wishful thinking will not make the problems go away. Although new ways of thinking can provide new choices, they are not necessarily ones which are politically, socially or personally easy to make; rather, the opposite. The deeper the problem, the more sweeping the required re-definitions, the greater the displacement of the status quo, and the stronger the resistance from those who have the authority to block re-definition. Paradoxically, the mechanism of change is least effective when change is most needed – when the stakes are high. The diagnostic indicators of the need for re-definition are the persistent failures of efforts to alter one of the conditions of the dilemma. When this happens it is time to try altering the assumption presenting the unacceptable choice.

Intellectually, it is easy to believe in the importance of re-definition and re-framing. We understand that we can be concept bound; that what we call something makes it what it is, and therefore constrains what we may do. New concepts, after they have been accepted, seem so simple and obvious that we often lose sight of how difficult is the process. The concept of the human "right" not to kill yourself working in order not to starve to death, in the form of child labor and occupational health and safety laws, took decades to accomplish and has an actual body count as a legacy. How could we have held on to the old concept of "management rights" for so long?

Concepts which are near and dear to vested ways of life are vigorously defended. The old concepts twist the alternatives into subordinate status and direct all energy to a steadfast "yes, but" position, rendering the need to change unnecessary.

In the search for the financial means to escape from the horns of the current dilemma, universities have not yet abandoned the hope that substantial increases in government funding may still be obtained through political action. The solution to our current problems will not come, however, until universities disabuse themselves of this belief. Whatever additional money comes from the amount of political pressure that realistically can be generated, given other social needs, will only briefly relieve the effects of past shortfalls. The extra money will not fix the buildings, re-equip the labs, reform the curriculum and cover a decade of future escalating salary costs.

Conclusions

The task is clear, but not simple. We must examine the assumptions and beliefs which have imprisoned us in our dilemmas, and then create a new way of thinking. As long as we continue to hold on to our current assumptions about the fundamental nature of the problems facing higher education, we will not find a solution.

We know that retrenchment results in either vertical or horizontal cuts which lose students, destroy programs and produce internal conflicts and lower morale. Yet it is the academic capacity to fill new roles and responsibilities which is necessary to avoid further retrenchment.

We know that sufficient additional funding is not going to be forthcoming from government, student fees or private industry to keep the status quo and to meet all the new expectations. Yet, moving forward into new areas requires a financial capacity and flexibility that does not exist.

We know that unless internal actions are taken, government intervention will be provoked in the form of abolishment of tenure, program-specific allocations and forced rationalization. Yet, the management capacity to engage the university community in a corporate commitment to change is lacking.

These three bad outcomes result from the way the current issues of higher education have been defined. This unhappy state of affairs is diagrammed in Figure 3-1 as the consequence which follows from the old assumptions, creating three negative outcomes, all of which compound the basic problems. There are only two ways out of such a dilemma:

First, either to persevere in trying to find politically possible ways of altering the outcomes resulting from the current definitions of the problems, such as generating additional funds through increasing student fees, but without it becoming counter productive by destroying good will and/or by provoking legislated cost-containment. The only reason to keep trying at this task is because of a fundamental belief that this is a coherent strategy. But the warning in 1980 was that these old ways will result in a house divided, as has been confirmed by Boyer's (1987) conclusion in *College*.

Or second, to re-define the problems based on new assumptions. We know that if we had academic flexibility we could hire new faculty to teach needed new material and close down dying areas. If we had financial flexibility we could buy new equipment, repair the crumbling plant and start new programs. And, if we had management flexibility arising from cooperation, good morale and lack of internal conflict we could achieve new roles and functions.

Therefore, the process of re-definition must begin by asking: what we would have to believe and think to re-define the situation in order to have academic, financial and management flexibility? I have used the phrase "The Assumption Gap" in Figure 3-1 as the label for this task. This book is about a changing our beliefs in a way that will re-define problems to provide the flexibility necessary to create a positive dynamic cycle.

In the next section, I will create the belief structure that is necessary. The beliefs I will present are consistent with my fundamental assumptions about history, economics, change and problem solving. They form coherent building blocks out of which to forge a viable prospect for the future of higher education.

The Assumption Gap: New Definitions of Problems Required to Reach Positive Ends

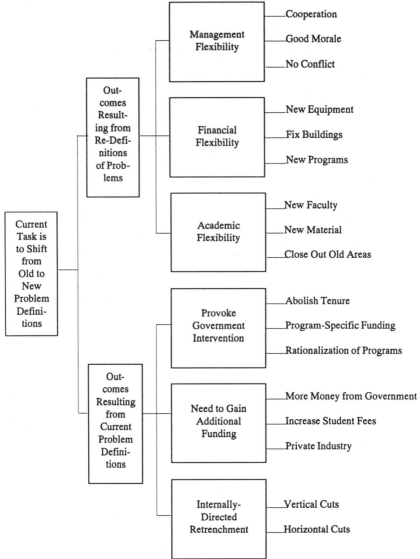

Old Assumptions

The consequences of traditional definitions of the problem are negative events which compound the difficulty, creating a negative cycle.

New Assumptions

The consequences of re-definition of the problem are positive events which create a positive dynamic cycle.

Section Two
Re-Defining Our
Beliefs

Section Two examines the beliefs which are required first to understand the current crisis in higher education and second to re-define the issues in new ways. I will present 24 bipolar dimensions. The beliefs at one end of each of the dimensions are used to describe the current issues of higher education. Beliefs at the opposite end of the dimensions re-define the issue in a way which will present new alternatives and options.

The 24 individual beliefs are grouped together to form ten higher order concepts. In turn, the ten concepts are organized into four chapters about people, change, academe and higher education respectively. The beliefs and their organization are summarized below:

Chapter 4: Beliefs About Ourselves
Our Circumstance
1. General/Specific
2. National/Local
3. External/Internal
Our Relationships
4. Them/Us
5. Passive/Active
Our Problems
6. Technical/Social
7. Product/Process
8. Symptom/Causes

Chapter 5: Beliefs About Change
Personal Change
9. Coercive/Constructive
10. Feasible/Acceptable

I refer to the beliefs at the poles of these dimensions as "templates" in order to emphasize that what people believe shapes the nature of events. However, because beliefs are changeable, relative and negotiable they are powerful means for altering reality by changing how we think. This philosophy of knowledge is in contrast to believing that it is reality which dictates our beliefs and that it is our task to discover what is real. When beliefs are seen to be reflections of objective reality, they become absolute "truths" and the only way to alter reality is to change the events themselves – events over which we often have very little control. It is often better and easier to alter our beliefs, over which we have a great deal of control, and in the process alter the nature of reality.

Chapter 4
Beliefs About Ourselves

It is our beliefs about ourselves and others which should be the starting point. The Carnegie Council in 1980 wrote:

We have an overall concern about higher education that transcends individual aspects. This is what may happen to the "private life" of the campus. This consists of the many personal relations among individuals and groups on campus, and the spirit and tone of the campus (p. 113).

The observation, a decade later, that we are a house divided (Boyer, 1987) without a sense of community (Carnegie Foundation, 1990a) is not the result of the public, government, university administration, faculty and students all being at cross-purposes. We are all on the same side; surely, this must be so. Therefore we must start with our beliefs about ourselves and our relationships with each other. How can we understand *our* mutual problem?

Our Circumstance

We have control over what we believe and how we act, but not over the beliefs of others on which they base their actions. Try as we might, it is a difficult task at best to make others do what we want them to do, and to have them match our expectations of them arising from our beliefs. However, if we assume that other people, like us, are reasonable and have good intentions, then the capacity to see their perspective also includes the possibility of creating new beliefs which rise above the impasse.

General/Specific

There is a sense, of course, in which events happening in remote spots of the world have a significant impact on higher education. The high energy costs resulting from the oil crisis contributed to accumulating operating deficits which, when combined with high interest rates, added significant new carrying charges to the operating budget. The falling levels of scholastic achievement made college teaching more difficult, brought critical attention to all of education at the very time colleges and universities were loading classes, inflating grades, deferring capital costs and raising tuition.

The lists could go on and on, as an incredible run of bad luck that hit higher education over the past decade. All of these are very general, and all are linked to other complex events, like the war in the Persian Gulf and performance in public schools across the nation, over which there is no clear access for influence. And, as some purists among academia would argue, rightly so.

There is truth in these general analyses. But there are also other truths, all very specific, and they are all things directly under the control and influence of the organization and structure of higher education.

Most universities have a senior faculty who are moving to the top of the salary scale. With steady state funding (increases which match inflation), itself unlikely, institutions face a 15% reduction in the size of their faculty, who are largely aging white males. At the same time, they will be required to teach an increasingly diverse group of students and will be called upon to meet changing national needs. These new roles and responsibilities are fitting less and less well with the skills of the existing professors who are not due to leave the university by normal attrition for another decade. Yet, there is neither the financial, academic nor management flexibility to respond. These are highly specific issues based on factors which were known well in advance – at least since 1980.

National/Local

The general issues on which we so often dwell are not just our problems; they are problems we share with others with whom we must work collectively to find resolutions through our common political and social mechanisms. As but one player, higher education must compete against the unorganized needs of the homeless and the organized efforts of the health establishment and others, for limited resources.

On a national scale, higher education may play out the same budget wars against "them" as academic departments do against each other. Higher education may even seek, at the state and national level, vertical cuts to eliminate other human services less essential than education, because the state government "cannot do everything for everyone;" yet strongly resist the same principle applied to their own curriculum as inappropriate because of the need to protect academic freedom, a value not shared by many external to the university. The price to continue fighting to do "well" on our terms will be to spend credibility and to draw on the reservoir of good will, provoking terms to be used against higher education such as *Prof-Scam* (Sykes, 1989) and *The Great Brain Robbery* (Bercuson, et al., 1984), all of which contain a sufficient element of the truth to be taken seriously by both ourselves and others.

Higher education will do relatively well in this national fight, but not as "well" as is required to **both** maintain the escalating costs of the status quo **and** to do all the new things which government, administration, faculty, students and public agree need to be done, now. I am not suggesting that we abandon our claim on the public purse. Everyone clearly understood the message of *A Nation at Risk* (National Commission, 1983). And, most important, everyone understands that higher education has not, and is not yet, doing its part in fixing the problem. It is instead "panhandling" for the additional resources, with "under-funding" as the buzz word, earning the disdain – appropriate or not – given to those who break the American work ethic.

What we have not been prepared to do is to take any significant local action which disrupt the status quo. As long as responsibility can be fixed at some other level, then it is easy to believe that the real problems are national or regional (i.e., State or Provincial governments) and that it is only the symptoms which are local.

External/Internal

By locating the problems as external, we within higher education are free to nag and complain. We expect someone else to take corrective actions for our problems. This is an uncomfortable position. This belief ties our fate to getting others to see us as their responsibility.

Not only are there specific local issues which are under the control and influence of the organization and structure of higher education, but many of them are also tied directly to the internal processes of every institution. They are the very processes into which individual faculty members not only have direct input, but, in fact, over which they have primary responsibility under the rules of faculty tradition and increasingly under collective bargaining. These are founded and defended as virtues based on principles of academic freedom.

But, the faculty no longer look to their own campus as their community. Most faculty derive their professional identity from their discipline. It is external peers who award prestige and confirmation through the recognition of grants and publications. Tight times have *en*trenched the importance of academic departments and disciplines in the struggles for self-preservation, manifest in budget wars, fought in World War I style of dug-in bottom lines.

Our Circumstance

Higher education must give up its belief that its current troubles are external, national and general. When we think in these terms, we will blame Government for breaking the faith, students for being too self-centred and unprepared, and a world economy for rendering our circumstances to the hapless chance of fate. The Carnegie Foundation's (1990a) study on *Campus Life* has shown morale to be low; faculty feel powerless because the causal conditions are believed to be external and largely beyond reach.

The alternative is to begin to see the troubles as internal, local and specific. These beliefs are empowering. They require nothing from others, but much of ourselves. Higher education is no longer a critical actor in a world-wide transformation into a new era. For many years colleges and universities have not been engaged in a continual renewal process that has allowed the tired to escape and to be replaced by a continuing flow into their ranks of irreverence and impatience. These are specific, local, internal issues.

Our Relationships

The current belief system of external, general and national sets "them" against "us," implying cross-purposes with those outside of higher education, and sets the sights of those inside higher education on the single-minded purpose of getting "them" to change. These are the perfect constructs for helplessness; higher education is without choice or direction, dependent on the actions of others to rescue its aspirations.

Attributions are powerful psychological processes. In tough times they provide the way people blame each other and claim the high ground for themselves. The fundamental attribution error is to excuse ourselves for shortcomings ("it was beyond my control") and to see shortcomings in others as a reflection of their true character. Social psychology has described this process in great detail.

Them/Us

Any view which dichotomizes the world into them versus us, the forces of darkness and light, of wrong and right, is a prescription for conflict. Yet every level of higher education is defining issues which divides players with a mutual stake into the opposing camps so clearly warned against in 1980 by the Carnegie Council: men/women, white/black, young/old, administration/faculty, students/faculty and university/government set against one another.

For example, the message to government and students has been to pay more. The *Chronicle of Higher Education* (Evangelauf, 1990a; 1991; 1992b) has reported for more than the past decade that tuition increases outpace inflation, and the issue of costs has become a recurring theme in the pages of *Change* (Langfitt, 1990; O'Keefe, 1987; Werth, 1988; Zemsky & Massy, 1990). The message back from government is to serve more, better, for the same or less money, or face increasing external interventions; these include discussions of exit standards as measured by achievement tests, scrutiny of the number of contact hours and the autonomy of professors (see Jacobson, 1992; Mooney, 1992), and calls for a legislated end to tenure as an outmoded concept no longer needed for the protection of freedom of thought and inappropriate as a protection against academic redundancy.

The ingredients for a classic epic struggle are all present. Casting higher education as the forces of light and governments (exemplified by Mrs. Thatcher) as the forces of darkness, the issues are clearly drawn. Robert Rosenzweig (1989) wrote that "intrinsically valuable intellectual work will languish and die if the test of the market is the main measure of their value." But, it is the perception within higher education that governments believe exactly in that test and no other (Shattock, 1989).

"Them" versus "Us" is a predictable prescription for conflict. Basic principles of social psychology tell us that both sides will become defensive. The script is to play a zero sum game. In the end both lose, when such an outcome serves the interests of neither.

Passive/Active

People are not passive or active by chance. People are passive when they do not feel that the actions they take have any actual effects. The current popular beliefs, held by those within higher education, in the general, national, external nature of the problems have left individuals with feelings of helplessness with respect to the external circumstances. Psychological research on helplessness has made clear that these conditions result in a mood and a mental state of "depression," which characterizes and helps to explain the withdrawn inward-looking state of current academic life.

In contrast, people actively direct their behavior when there are perceived and real contingencies between what they do and outcomes. Contingencies are powerful controllers of human behavior. Contingencies in the minds of some are authoritarian and arbitrary; but that is a foolish view. It is not a matter of whether contingencies will influence our relations with each other, but rather what they shall be and how they shall be determined. Higher education does not have to look beyond the campus to begin examining the contingencies between outcomes and what people do.

If keeping a faculty job requires a research paper, then a research paper it will be; it will not be helping an undergraduate learn to write, when that was the job of "them," the public schools anyway. Contingencies direct the behavior and the rationalization follows: "It is not my fault I have to make this choice between teaching and research, because it is caused by the poor performance and lack of action by ill-advised others, including the student." This is the primary attribution error and The Carnegie Foundation (1989) faculty surveys have captured the growing "blame the student" attribution process.

Our Relationships

We know quite a lot about people and how they relate to each other. Often it is far easier to change the contingencies in the situation than try to blame or change persons. Often it is the situation which is the problem, not the motivations of the person.

Although competition has served higher education well, in many ways, over its period of growth and expansion, the structures and procedures put in place over this period are no longer serving higher education well. Competition in situations of negative growth breeds a self-centred life-boat mentality. Such is human nature. We may try to change human nature by appeals for community, commonality and sharing. However, appeals to such popularly acknowledged values have been with us at least as long as organized religion, attempting to redress man's inhumanity to man with little effect. There is no reason to believe such appeals will work now to redress campus life.

Successful cooperatives, as one example, have non-competitive rules by which members may best advance their own interest through the well-being of the whole. We do not have such a corporate culture within higher education, which provides the contingencies to actively draw us, collectively, into problem-solving modes. Rather, we are encouraged to be passive about critical issues and to see others as responsible. Part of the process of re-definition is to gain a new perspective on our relationships by creating contingencies that will support active cooperative relationships.

Our Problems

Assuming ownership of a problem is difficult. If authority for action is up to someone else, we escape responsibility, but also freedom. Only by accepting responsibility for our personal roles and our contributions to difficulties can we gain the freedom of choice and self-direction. We have known this, too, for years; it is just very difficult. For higher education to approach this ideal it is first necessary to change its beliefs; then, and only then, can it become responsible for determining its own consequences through its own choices.

Technical/Social

One of the common myths about the great social problems of our times is of their intractableness. The belief that social problems are so complex and so deeply ingrained as to defy solution is simply wrong. Most, if not all, the basic elements are well understood and there are many direct technical solutions which are feasible and affordable. The problems are "difficult" and "intractable" only because each of the feasible solutions is unacceptable to some group having the wealth or power to block its implementation, usually because they will lose privilege in the process.

So cast, issues take on a different character when seen from the perspective of whose sensibilities will be offended, as distinct from the question of whether some strategy is technically feasible. Their name notwithstanding, "social" issues are seldom openly debated on the level of acceptability. The argument that a particular solution should not be considered because it is offends "my" status is not an acceptable currency of intellectual exchange. Thus, the self-interest agenda remains hidden, and technical difficulties are put forward as the "real" problem while the critical obstacle of people remains invisible.

Over the past few decades we have solved the technical difficulties associated with some very complex problems – including going into and coming from space. Fixing the learning problems associated with retention of nontraditional students, the absence of appropriate real world experiences in the curriculum, or even strategies for cost containment are far less difficult and certainly less expensive in direct costs. The reasons we do not solve these problems have to do with our social and psychological nature, and the fact that our efforts are directed more at the technical difficulties of feasibility and less at the fundamental problem of acceptibility. The problems of higher education are social problems.

Product/Process

Ten people wish to divide themselves into two evenly matched teams of five to play a basketball game. Of the more than 200 possibilities, which is the best alignment? That is a product type of question for which an endless Senate-style academic debate could consume the entire time set aside for the game. However, two roughly equivalent players can take turns picking the players for their team and achieve one of the many possible desirable combinations in less than a minute. This is a process solution. It is one in which the final outcome (the product) can not be known or predicted in advance, but can result in evenly matched teams with a high degree of reliability (certainly higher than a ten person group discussion and a consensus decision).

Dilemmas persist when people keep searching for the "right" answer, a product. For example, which departments should absorb a retrenchment of one position to balance the budget now (as opposed to later which is implied for the next round of budget cuts)? This is much like the choice between being shot or hanged, or the choice between self-imposed retrenchment or government intervention. There is no "right" answer to requests for such choices. Higher education cannot pick whether the computer for one is more important than the books for another, any more than people can rationally pick in times of famine who should eat and who should starve. At some point, the only possibility for an escape is shifting the discussion from: "Which choice shall we make?" to "How are we going to solve this problem?" The frequent actual response in colleges and universities has been the pronouncement: "We have to set priorities," meaning begin the game of budget wars (i.e., fight over who should starve). This is using product thinking when a process is required.

Causes/Symptoms

Someone said "A hen is an egg's way of making another egg." In the same sense, retrenchment (cutting back what we do) causes financial restraint (our need to cut back). We do not live in a linear world. The alternatives available often take new shapes when what was seen as a cause of a problem – such as lack of money – is recast as a symptom of a more basic cause, such as not having a suitable and appropriate product.

Each of the major issues facing higher education can be stood on its head. The result is seldom comfortable, as when students not learning is seen as the symptom, the obvious focus shifts attention to the teacher as the cause. As professors, we have little control over the multitude of social, economic and political factors of which, for better or worse, the twenty-something generation are a product; but we do have a great deal of control over ourselves.

Our Problems

To say, as I have just done, that our problems are our beliefs is not to deny the existence of real financial, academic and management problems and the need for practical solutions of them. It is simply to say that serious problems which seem impossible to solve are, in fact, the very ones for which solutions will not come the harder we try to discover the correct technical answer. Rather, they are primarily problems for which higher education must first examine its own beliefs in order to find ways to re-define the issues.

Conclusions

None of these beliefs are original. The effects of each are well grounded in individual and social psychology. They are, however, a useful check list to apply whenever people have the subjective experience of being in a dilemma. True dilemmas will never be solved by discovering the correct, or even the "more" correct, of two incompatible alternatives. Under such conditions, the choice will reflect the relative power and wealth of the players and will be temporary in nature. True dilemmas are only solved by re-definition, which inevitably shifts power and wealth, and is a difficult adjustment for people to make because those who must change will often be negatively affected by the outcome.

However, a re-definition of the difficulties in higher education as specific, local and internal will allow us to stop blaming others and give us the capacity to take an active role with others in finding solutions. The demands placed upon us are social in nature, because we must look for process which will allow us to see current problems as the symptoms and to seek their causes at other levels of analysis.

Chapter 5
Beliefs About Change

Our understanding of the process of change is an extrapolation based in part on our analysis and conceptualization of changes in the past, and in part on our own experiences. But, these are two very different levels of analysis. The first uses historical and the second psychological templates.

Historically, the focus is on events marking inflection points which change the course of human existence, such as illustrated by Darwin's theory of evolution. Labelling inflection points in history is always arbitrary, at best, and linking them with the iconoclasts most responsible for them must of necessity be an oversimplification of complex events converging at a particular moment in time. However, by whatever yardstick is used, the number of years between historical inflection "points" has shrunk dramatically. The emergence of the agricultural era spans thousands of years, the industrial era hundreds of years and the atomic era perhaps only decades.

Thus, like everything else, the process of change is itself changing. For the purpose of this monograph, we need a way of thinking about change which is appropriate for the kinds of issues now facing higher education.

Inflection Points

Darwin's contribution of natural selection provides a good example of the necessity of changing the way we now think about change. It is a familiar concept and it is consistent with the assumption made in Chapter 3 that now is an epochal period.

Biological Evolution

Survival of the fittest as a biological concept was useful to explain adjustments made over eons of time. But, as humans evolved and began to control their environment, rather than being controlled by it, this concept became less useful for explaining the connections from the immediate past to the present. The rate of change affecting human adaptations has exceeded the speed of the mechanism of natural selection.

Cultural Evolution

The logical extension of biological evolution was cultural evolution: the survival of those institutions and traditions which were adaptive to social, economic and political conditions. For the Modern Era, the one just concluded, change was a social evolutionary process occurring over generations and ending with us in the democratic industrial state. But, as the required adjustments are increasingly shifting, from those to which human kind reacted, to those that human kind creates, there is a need for still another refinement.

Psychological Evolution and the Post-Modern Person

Although the post-modern era that we are now beginning is often referred to as the "Information Age" – with an emphasis on technology – this is a different template than one which extends Darwin's concept of evolution. As Roger Walsh (1984) has put forth in his book, *Staying Alive*, for the first time in human history most of the threats to human existence have been created by human beings who are still alive. Collectively, from now on, every person is the potential author of their own fate. Thus, the post-modern adaptations for human survival are personal and psychological in nature. The significant epochal nature of this period, as it affects finding solutions to the many social problems now facing us – including those of higher education – will depend upon a set of highly personal and social beliefs for viewing change. Used as templates, these beliefs forcefully direct attention toward very particular ways of thinking and acting.

Personal Change

Now more than ever before, the principle dimensions for understanding acceptance of and resistance to change requires an internal reference point anchored in the individual. This is not to deny that science and technology are the driving force requiring change, nor that the integration of science, technology and society is arguably the central issue of our time. But simply that it is the psychology of the individual that now must become central. The pressure for adaptation is not **between** generations, but **within** individuals. "Psychological Darwinism," the survival of "self," becomes the replacement term for biological (species) and cultural (institutions) evolution.

We now know better the importance of the phrase of the 1960s, "the future is now." We must re-define how we relate to each other and how our political and social institutions work now, or there will not be a future for us, those who are now living. This requires discarding the values and beliefs toward which we have already made a commitment of self through the process of living out part of our lives; these are central beliefs which, mid-stream in life, are no longer appropriate. Thus, discarding them invalidates in an important sense our very existence. Change is now something we must do for ourselves, not something we do to benefit our children.

Individual psychological survival now requires a new sense of self, one anticipated by George Kelly (1955) in his book *The Psychology of Personal Constructs*. Kelly proposed that we use our beliefs (which he called personal constructs) to anticipate events. When events do not match our expectations, we experience threat because we have lost our capacity to predict and thus control what happens to us.

What we have not yet learned is how to live this philosophy of discarding outdated central beliefs about self within a lifetime. Kelly warned us that when our constructs fail and we feel threatened, that we seek certainty, and that we often try to preserve our beliefs by trying to force events to fit our existing constructs. Humanistic accomplishment, however, occurs when we can rise above the subjective sense of threat – arising from having self invalidated – to regain control by re-definitions through new beliefs which capture a new reality.

Coercive/Constructive

The subjective experience of threat, which results from a breakdown in the usefulness of an individual's constructs (i.e., beliefs), is the basis for human dilemmas, which lead to one of two possible choices.

The coercive choice is to restore coherence by using force or authority to make events comply with our expectations. Parents do this often, with a glare or a whack, adjusting the child's behavior to match the parent's constructions of what their child is like. Sometimes, of course, such constructions are quite useful; a flash of muscle keeps a less useful "childish" construct from intruding into the mature world. At other times, the show of force is itself the coercive act, captured in classic form by the General in Vietnam who said "unfortunately we had to destroy the village in order to save it."

The constructive choice is to abandon inappropriate constructions and adopt new ones, as does the scientist, who in the face of clear negative evidence seeks alternative theoretical constructs. For Kelly, the "humanistic dilemma" was knowing when to hold fast to an existing definition, and when to engage in the process of re-definition. The "human tragedy" was the ensuing struggle between those who seek to preserve the status quo against those who wish to impose a new alternative definition. Most significant human accomplishments, such as the civil and human rights movement, have a real body count to bear witness to the struggle, e.g., Martin Luther King and, in a symbolic way, all of the freedom riders who were spat upon.

Feasible/Acceptable

For all of the teachings of organized religion over time, "love sweet love" is a feasible solution to most if not all of the world's problems; but, it is not acceptable. When too much effort is spent trying to find the correct answer (a product, such as which department to drop as a vertical cut), the focus will invariably be on whether my definitions are better than yours, making it harder to re-define the issues in ways that are acceptable to both parties. The tougher the problem, the more essential it is to look at the personal investments each party has to their particular definitions and what it is which renders specific outcomes as acceptable or not. These are human problems, and the issues in higher education are much more about what is acceptable than they are about what is feasible.

Organizational Change

The beliefs used for describing individuals and modern change have their parallel in conceptualizing change within organizations. Too much conceptual emphasis is placed on social and organizational structures acting in a "rational" manner. Indeed, the term often applied by government to the issue of cost-containment in higher education systems is "rationalization" of special roles and functions between campuses or institutions. When the same philosophy is applied locally it comes out as the phrase that "this institution cannot be all things to all people; it is time to set priorities," implying rational choices.

However, we must remember that institutions do not have emotions or minds, only people do. Institutions are not rational, nor do they make decisions. People make decisions which are more or less rational as we understand that term from economics. What is rational for a given person may or may not be rational for the collective. When decision making is de-centralized and when compliance is largely invisible and un-monitored – as it is in teaching and research (and in policing, doctoring and a shrinking but identifiable number of occupations) – "rational" institutional behavior is a dysfunctional perspective; it is the misapplication of an economic concept where social and psychological ones are more appropriate.

With new forms of change comes the need for new management styles. American business copied Japanese management styles, and higher education is now trying to copy American business (e.g., Gardner, Warner & Biedenweg, 1990). In fact, both business and higher education should be trying to develop new terms of reference for a new period based on new principles – those based on social psychology and the psychology of the individual. Indeed, the translation and application of "Quality Management" and "Re-engineering" concepts to higher education will require such a perspective if they are to be successful.

Secondary/Primary

A secondary change is one which makes adjustments. It is the type of change associated with reform and the one with which we are most familiar. A problem comes up, a solution is introduced, and business returns to normal in a somewhat different way. In the old days, management was responsible for the identification and definition of problems, solutions and implementations. In modern times, the entire process has become more participatory, due to recognition of the simple fact that those closest to the action often know both first and best.

Such participation and openness, however, should not confuse the difference between shared and actual power. Lee Iacocca (1984) did believe that the "buck stops here;" that he was responsible for a corporate objective of quality that all employees can relate to, believe in and become committed to. A lot of the details of how to do this are negotiable and participatory, particularly those where Lee does not know best, but not the ones which Lee knows that Lee knows best.

Primary change is far different. In simple terms, it is a process where the outcome will disrupt existing power and authority. It is one where the outcome may well be that some of the issues that Lee knows that Lee knows best are also negotiable, including Lee himself. It is for this reason that Kuhn (1970) described paradigm shifts in science as "revolutions." Primary change involves not only the currency of the ideas (i.e., is this re-definition better), but also the politics of power. When primary change took eons, or even centuries, the changing of the guard was between generations, not within a generation as it is now.

As with using any belief as a template, forcing issues into dichotomous distinctions can be dangerous if they lead to either/or thinking, rather than relative emphasis. Of course, in times of change both secondary and primary processes are going on together. As an example, in the current search for social justice and racial harmony there is generational change. If we could wait for the reform of enlightened education of our children to have its effect, in 100 years racism will not be a problem. However, the need for this transformation has out-paced this secondary change time-frame. Too much is happening too fast in terms of the changing racial composition of the nation. In the decade of the 1990s, the institutions of this nation will discover racial tolerance out of economic necessity; and in the process, individuals – particularly those of us who are white – will need to change themselves in the primary ways of sharing wealth, power and the authority to define what is legitimate.

Successive/Simultaneous

When the rate of change was slower it was possible to manage change; to see it as a linear and successive set of cause-effect steps to get from point A to point B, such as Planning, Organizing, Actualizing (mobilizing the organizational climate) and Evaluation. The modern management by objectives philosophy of redrawing the flow chart from a line to a circle, with evaluation forming a feedback loop to inform planning, was only a secondary change.

Yet, university planning processes are still dominated by the need to begin with a mission statement, whether or not it matches individual agendas. There is the mistaken belief that the resulting statement is somehow an expression of a pure product rather than simply the end point of a political process dictated by the power of the status quo. Although the process may be based on debate, the outcome need not be "rational." The article of faith behind the mission statement is still the old one of a beginning point from which change and the authority to manage change flows.

Primary change is the simultaneous coming together of multiple levels of analysis and processes. Organizations do not do this well. An organizational sub-unit that must implement a change, must use the means it has available, which is often part of the problem needing to be changed. The result is contradiction. For example, the teaching and learning process is largely in the hands of individual faculty in discipline-based departments, who cannot fundamentally change what they do (e.g., start reading student writing) without disrupting their own lives (e.g., such as their discipline and department-based research career) in which they have a heavy investment of self. As different learners – rather than new learners – come to the university for new and different purposes, it will not be possible now to add a new generation of faculty to be their teachers, as was possible in 1960. Simultaneous requires a non-linear mind-set.

Conclusions

It is paradoxical that both individuals and individual institutions are both more and less important than in the past. In some ways, as we move toward a world community, each has less and less control over their lives. There is much less access to influence conditions which affect them than was true, not that long ago, when the boundaries of the village (or campus) set the limit on the majority of events that had a daily direct personal impact. Now, change is so pervasive that it out-races biological and cultural evolution, and has at least as much impact on persons as on organizations and institutions. In fact, as organizations and institutions attempt to adapt, they become the instruments for delivering the burdens of change which are placed on individuals. The person is more central than ever.

Higher education, as an establishment, is under pressure to change and adapt, but as it attempts to do so, additional burdens are placed on the faculty, students and administrators to make the very choices which will disrupt their lives. The process of change no longer primarily pits one generation against another, i.e., one "intact" self using the political structure of the organization to impose one version of truth over another. Now, no person can have a life-long commitment which will see them out. We must all change often. This has never happened before in the history of humankind. Increasingly, our use of concepts from economics and organizational behavior must give way to re-definitions which are based on the psychology of individuals. Paradox and dilemma are states of the mind. Our beliefs are central, and it is time to re-think how we think about the changes that are now required.

Chapter 6
Beliefs About Academic Life

The goals of higher education do not come in handy units. Unlike most goods and services, the capacity to use the mind to create new ideas, new knowledge and new applications, and to teach this skill to others, is hard to measure. The currency of exchange for academic life is elusive, yet it is necessary for deciding such things as what courses to offer, which ones are to be required, which faculty to promote, and to arrange the teaching and learning experience into a curriculum. It should not be surprising that life in the world of ideas often seems to involve paradox and contradictions, due simply to the elusive and intangible nature of the products of teaching, public service and research, and the disjointed expectations of the students who receive the teaching, the government which pays for it and the disciplines which set the standards.

The World of Ideas

When he was President of Stanford University, Donald Kennedy used a metaphor from philosophy of science when he suggested that a "new paradigm" – which has now become a buzz-word in higher education – is necessary in order to re-frame the purpose and organization of higher education, and that it would require "revolutionary" changes (Grassmuck, 1990a). Kennedy's reference was to Thomas Kuhn's (1970) description of scientific progress as being marked by periodic "revolutions" followed by refinement (i.e., reform). It is a useful caricature of academic life which operates with the dual currencies of *ideas* and *brokerage*.

It is unfortunate, however, that the word "revolution" has such strong negative connotations, for much of what we call humanistic accomplishment has been achieved only through a political struggle to introduce new ways of thinking, and with the ideas, new people who then come to control the establishment. Most academics have no higher dream than to have a revolutionary idea, a concept or idea so penetrating that it changes the direction of thought and establishes them in a position of influence.

The brokerage of power in academic life is only occasionally revealed. Arthur Koestler, in his book *The Call Girls*, captures this side of academic life with an account of male academics at a conference placing personal advancement over the advancement of knowledge. In *The Case of the Midwife Toad*, he described the power of the modern scientific establishment to suppress heretical ideas, not unlike what Galileo experienced at the hands of the church.

Reform/Revolution

Examples of people who have had a revolutionary influence are Galileo, Darwin and Freud, to mention a few who have left a mark on human thought that has cut across disciplines and decades. But, there are many smaller theories and concepts, specific to a discipline for a short time span, in which the person leaves a mark, sometimes even a piece of equipment (e.g., in psychology a Skinner box) which imposes conceptual constraints on ideas by virtue of a method. Little academic revolutions are going on all the time. Often several combine to form the ingredients necessary for a much larger one, ushering in a new vocabulary and new view. The 1990s are revolutionary times. Changes are going on in every discipline, and they are converging to form larger movements that are shaking the establishment, as well they should. The current world of ideas has been in the hands of its current brokers for 30 years now, with low levels of renewal (Bowen & Schuster, 1986). Exciting times should be ahead.

From a revolutionary perspective, the appropriate discourse should be over the values, philosophy and concepts which shall constitute the legitimate authority for the definition and standards of accountability, it should not be over procedures, techniques and products. Yet it is the reform implied by the latter that occupies the attention of higher education: how those who are on the inside can do better what they already do, not what else is to be done by who else. Reform and revolution are two very different processes.

Collectively, higher education has not accepted the perspective that these are revolutionary times. With the impending faculty shortage resulting from a lost generation of scholars, combined with the end to mandatory retirement in the U.S., the realistic prospect is for another decade or more of the status quo. As short as is a decade in the grand sweep of human events, responding to the new challenges is unlikely to wait for even that long. With the accelerating rate of social change, the magnitude of change in the past century perhaps may be equalled in the next decade. Revolutionary change is now within, not between, generations.

Competition/Cooperation

The unusual importance placed on civility in the academic culture is for good reason; intense competition is just below the surface. It begins with a long selection process. Until very recently, less than half attended college, a small proportion sought graduate training, less than half of whom were accepted, less than half of those completing the PhD, and less than half who sought to be admitted to academe were accepted, with grants, publications and peer recognition limited to far less than half of those. It should not be surprising that academic life is reported to be a source of considerable personal strain (Carnegie Foundation, 1989), and in the words of the Carnegie Foundation (1990b) that "there is blunt evidence that those who would retire early are disenchanted with their professional experience to date."

Richard Elmore (1989) wrote "what we do is what we teach." Our examples speak louder than words, and the world of ideas is extremely competitive. Yet most of life – working within a business and living within a relationship – requires cooperation. It is not that we do not know how to make the process of teaching and learning a cooperative process; we understand full well that it requires the integration of community and learning (Astin, 1987; Palmer, 1987; Wagner, 1987). The problem is, there are simply few structures for its exemplification, and there will not be many without revolutionary changes.

Russell Edgerton (1989), reflecting on the agenda of AAHE over the past few years, asked the rhetorical question "Why don't we teach better?" His reply was that there is a need to "re-structure" and "re-define" what we do and how we do it. Higher education already understands the critical issues requiring re-definition and re-structuring. What is lacking is the capacity to act on them precisely *because* the solutions require *re*-definition and *re*-structuring. Genuine re-definition and re-structuring shift power and control and are revolutionary in nature; such are the implications of seeking the "new paradigm."

The addition of more women is one revolutionary force through feminist philosophy, as women's ways of knowing through relationships penetrate academe (Belenky, et al., 1986). Further, new views of academic leadership are being expressed by women who are college and university presidents, which reflect feminist ways of thinking (Bensimon, 1991; Shalala, 1989) and the observation that women excel as campus citizens (Carnegie Foundation, 1990c).

To pretend that the world of ideas is "objective," "value free" and "impersonal" is sheer nonsense. There is a culture of academic life, expressed at each specific institution in the specific way faculty and students interact, that shape and directs what is considered legitimate and proper, and what will and will not be tolerated (Tierney, 1988, 1991). The contradiction arises from the myth of a community of scholars, openly and freely exchanging ideas in a non-coercive search of knowledge, but one in which each person, at the same time, is in competition with the next. The world of ideas is an extremely competitive business and it has developed its own industry.

The Industry of Ideas

The industry of ideas requires three beliefs that can be used as templates for viewing academic life: the role of the disciplines and professions, the relative importance of people and situations, and the responsibilities of administrators entrusted with orchestrating the isolated pieces.

Bureaucratic & Professional/Community

The rapid expansion of higher education in both the United States (Carnegie Council, 1980) and Canada (Leslie, 1980; Symons & Page, 1984), drew on a similar pool of scholars and has a common ideology, thus creating similar current conditions in both countries. In particular, the faculty age distribution, which has already been discussed, has the joint economic and academic aspects of escalating salary costs and a closed system. The resulting challenges, respectively, are the loss of financial and academic flexibility. However, the rapid expansion which gave rise to these issues also has had far-reaching organizational implications for academic life and its management. Jencks and Riesman (1969) used the title *The Academic Revolution* to describe what was taking place in the 1960s; it was indeed a "revolution" as I am using the term.

Major research universities expanded their PhD programs, and other colleges and universities joined in the process as fast as they were able. Young PhDs, trained as researchers, competed for the expanding academic positions in institutions with PhD programs. The remainder settled elsewhere in the liberal-arts colleges, bringing the culture and ethic of their graduate training with them. Their institutions adopted the ethic as well, in part by providing research facilities in order to compete in attracting new faculty, and by actively encouraging researchers to compete among themselves for national prestige, using the common currency of the times. This part of higher education became institutionalized; it found expression in individual colleges and universities, which provided the settings for the modern ethic of academic life. The result was, as Jencks and Riesman noted, a group of individuals "responsible primarily to themselves and their colleagues rather than their employers and committed to the advancement of knowledge rather than any particular institution."

Rau and Becker (1989) have carried this analysis forward to the present, describing the modern manifestations as increasing bureaucratization and professionalization. In this atmosphere, the campus-community has atrophied in comparison to the discipline-community. Paradoxically, the very organizational structures set up to promote excellence have acted contrary to the conditions most necessary for effective teaching and learning. The faculty reward system has narrowed at the very time in history that the need for greater variation and cross-discipline interaction was expanding (Boyer, 1990). There is, in the terms of the theme of the 1993 national conference of the American Association of Higher Education, a need to "re-discover community."

Person/Situation

An analogy for academic life, to which I will return later, is with policing. Policemen, like academics, traditionally had individual control over how they did their work, which was largely invisible to their supervisors. However, the modern technology of a video camera on the hood of the patrol car or in the hands of an observer makes this less true than it used to be. But, perhaps it is simply a forerunner of academic accountability in the information age.

It has never been clear from the police literature whether the problem of the excessive use of force was because policemen tended to have authoritarian personalities or because the nature of policing and the police organization promoted and supported such behaviors. The relative emphasis placed on person-centred versus situation-centred explanations has considerable importance for how issues are defined and what are considered appropriate solutions, e.g., to change police recruitment and training to get less violent men, or to change the quasi-military nature of the organization which supports authoritarian behavior. Despite considerable evidence for the latter, the police establishment has spent most of its efforts on the former.

In academic life, bureaucratization and professionalization are two of the formal mechanisms for civility and for sheltering individual entrepreneurism and its competitive nature. However, until this is more openly recognized, serious distortions can be introduced into the explanations offered for the problems and issues of higher education and the interventions required. For example, appeals to individuals for better teaching will have little effect when the situation does not support the activity. When competition and entrepreneurism is highly valued, cooperation and relationships are undermined, lip service to the contrary values notwithstanding.

The contradiction of the emphasis on person over the primacy of the situation has its purpose. In competition, there can only be a limited number of winners, so it is necessary for the faculty member who does not win national acclaim, or the student who fails, to accept personal responsibility for their failure. William Ryan (1971), in his classic work, has called this *Blaming the Victim*, for which we have institutionalized the process which insulates the winners by helping the losers to assume responsibility for the authorship of their own misfortune. To shift attention to the situation would be to invite the revolution of systemic change, rather than the reforms of secondary change which leave those with position and authority still at the helm.

Manager of Change/Agent of Change

In the previous period of change of the 1960s, when there was clear external support for the role and function of higher education – justice and equality through education and to be first in science and technology – it was safe for colleges and universities to take risks and to experiment. As a result, an academic revolution took place. However, when universities are under attack, as they are today, to do more and better with less, there is a natural defensive response. On the one hand, the survivors of individual entrepreneurism wish to protect the status quo, and on the other hand, there is an incapacity for the critics to act, because the mechanisms and values required to protect irreverence do not permit direct political intrusions. As Howard Bowen (1983) insightfully noted early in the process of retrenchment, although selective cutting is widely acclaimed it is little practised, while across the board cuts, which are seldom advocated, are widely practised. The mechanisms for intrusive change do not exist; some critics argue they should be added, primarily through the elimination of tenure (e.g., Bercuson, et al., 1984; Sykes, 1989).

In academe, there is not much muscle for making the tough decisions for which the commercial world prides itself, and for good reason; but, there is no denying that the same good reasons makes managing internal change difficult. The growing emergence of the phrase "management rights" in contract negotiations is an example of seeking to give administrators and the boards of governors the power many of those on the outside believe they need to manage change. But, change can not be managed in this way because of how the academy is organized against such intrusions. Thus, the internal problem is that the challenge of change is threatening to the status quo of the existing culture, and administrators require the support of that culture as the source of their authority.

The paradox is that the conditions blocking the intrusion of administrative authority for managing change are the very ones that allow change to challenge that authority and the status quo. The very lack of explicit power to manage change is also the license for the outrageous. This is the role for an agent provocateur. Those mechanisms which serve to protect civilized competition and insulate irreverence need to be used to create change. Efforts to manage significant change will fly in the face of tradition and will be blocked, but theoretically, significant change can thrive, provided it comes from within.

Administrators are caught between these two forces of needing to be both managers and agents of change at the same time. This distinction will be more fully developed in Chapter 10. Clearly, if significant change does not come from within, it will soon come from without. If it is to come from within, administrators must shift their roles and responsibilities from being a manager of change to an agent of change – of unleashing the power of the organization on itself. To expect administrators to manage change that is required in epic proportions is to ask for the impossible, unless external intrusions by government first alter the system.

Conclusions

Academic life in the world and industry of ideas perhaps has no parallel. Although intensely competitive, academe attempts to be extremely civil, insulating individuals from intrusions of others. It is hard to disrupt the status quo, but theoretically, it is also hard to stop creative, different and innovative ideas. This ideal of academe, however, has started to break down as existing structures which were designed to protect radical thought have been diverted to protect the status quo in response to shrinking resources. As a result, the innovative and heretical have been shut out from the inside. The conflict has started to erupt beyond the boundaries of control historically provided by internal tradition and etiquette. Efforts to manage change have been ineffective because the structures which insulate academics from intrusions prevent change from being imposed by others. But, significant change will come. If that change is to come as an internal, self-directed revolution, rather than be externally imposed, then the very structures which are now insulating the status quo need to become the mechanisms for change. Increasingly, administrators will need to exercise their positions to be internal agents of change, more than managers of change.

Chapter 7
Beliefs About Higher Education

The last chapter presented beliefs for thinking about the individual colleges and universities where specific faculty and students come together under the leadership of administrators at specific campuses. This chapter presents beliefs for thinking about the "Institution" of higher education as a North American "Establishment." Collectively, individual colleges and universities are a loose federation, subject to similar external economic conditions and national educational policies, and bound together through common associations and philosophies. These beliefs have to do with money, goals and governance; these are the three issues that form the three major challenges to higher education as an Establishment.

Means

Many of the current issues of higher education centre around money. On the supply end are the size of yearly increases in tuition, government grants and incidental user-pay fees. On the demand end are salaries, maintenance and new courses and forms of teaching arising from a new and increasingly diverse clientèle in terms of age, race, gender, ability and personal motivation.

Under-Funded/Over-Extended

Act I of the politics of higher education has been for university presidents and other spokespersons to talk of "under-funding" as the basic starting point – the bottom line has been that the increase in funding this year is less than the inflationary increase of university expenses and the need for new programs. Once this position is taken, it is necessary to list all of the dire consequences that will follow as Act II; in particular, the dangers to the national agenda of economic competitiveness in a world economy because of an undertrained work force. This has not been an effective threat. Governments actually decreased appropriations for 1992-93 (Jaschik, 1992), and industry (Eurich, 1985; Wallace, 1990) and community colleges (Collison, 1991b) are absorbing the learning requirements for continuing education and for the training and re-training of the work force. Re-alignments to meet the new needs without new amounts of money are under way. Act III is in the process of being written.

Specific scenes from Act II of the drama are to take students as hostages by calculating the size of the compensatory fee increase required to cover the shortfall, as happened across the United States in the 1990/1991 academic year when 30 states made mid-term budget reductions (Cage, 1991) and more cuts were forecast for 1991-92 in a state-by-state review (Blumenstyk & Cage, 1991). For example, the President of the Pennsylvania State University was quoted as saying that "it was a reasonable assumption" that tuition would be raised beyond the anticipated 6% if the state offered a smaller funding increase (Center Daily Times, Feb. 6, 1991). Often the hostages could be counted upon to march on statehouses and to hold public demonstrations, as did the Penn State students, sometimes gaining national publicity as did the demonstrations by the students from SUNY and CUNY (Blumenstyk, 1991; *Newsweek*, April, 29, 1991). The closing lines of this scene accused government of lack of leadership, poor vision and bad faith as did the president of the Canadian Association of University Teachers (Smith, 1989).

In fact, neither the public nor the government is anti-education. There is extraordinary faith in the U.S. and Canada on the value of higher education. How refreshing it would be to hear someone in a position of authority simply say that we are over-extended, it is quite clear how it happened and no one in particular is to blame; and then to proceed on the assumption that all parties are willing to make a constructive effort at problem solving if given half a chance. For many, the term "under-funded" is simply inappropriate in comparison to other demands, as is the process of drawing battle lines between good (us) and bad (them) guys.

Retrenchment / Dynamism

Retrenchment is a process; it has principles and it works in known ways. It is a reactive process which feeds on itself. Once the belief of under-funding is used as the template to define the problem, then the enemy is identified and the required cuts can be done with clean hands by helpless internal administrators. However, any cut, by definition, reduces the capacity to provide some services and runs the risk of contributing to the need for further retrenchment. For example, many universities resorted to faculty and staff lay-offs in response to the most recent reductions (Mangan, 1991). In Florida, the mid-year reductions of 91-92 were achieved by non-replacement of faculty and by offering fewer courses, which resulted in a 2.3% drop in enrollment and a short fall of tuition revenue producing a new deficit (*St. Petersburg Times*, December 11, 1992).

Retrenchment is a very powerful word which, when used as a template, preempts the problem-solving process. Often what follows is a discussion of the relative merits of vertical or horizontal cuts, as if the problem had been adequately defined and now there is a clear choice to be made. However, a slow death by starvation or a quick stab in the back are not fundamentally different. Both arise from conflict and a life-boat mentality. Retrenchment is strong evidence of poor problem solving when the only choice is between unacceptable alternatives and the only available process is prioritizing them.

Dynamism is the opposite; it is not a fairy tale of some ideal that we all want. Often someone says to me, "we are *all* for dynamism," implying that I naïvely fail to understand that "retrenchment" is reality and dynamism is fantasized thinking. It is not a matter of wishing for dynamism, like a winning lotto ticket; it is created. It is a pro-active process that also has principles and works in known ways.

When things start to get tough it is time to use the belief of dynamism as the template. The issue is not what can be cut, but what of the available resources can be re-directed or re-invested toward other ends. If you are for "dynamism," then you do find a way for the arts centre to survive by linking its roles and functions with those of others in common purpose, and you do not rank the business school as more important so that it may be sustained this year at its present level from the savings recovered from the cannibalized line from theatre, especially when the lost line will assure fewer and poorer university theatre performances and larger user-pay shortfalls in that department.

A hungry circle of cannibals does not yield constructive group problem solving. There are such things as self-perpetuating loops, one of which is the negative cycle from the process of retrenchment, and another is the positive cycle from that of dynamism. The former might appear superficially easier because the up-front choice is a quick fix of real dollars, but the long-term effect is expensive. The latter is immediately more difficult, but the back-end gains are large and re-claim the future.

Ends

What is the purpose of higher education? There is no consensus on the answer to that question because each possible answer rests on different – often only implicit – assumptions (e.g., Barber, 1992; Barnett, 1990; Bok, 1990). Thus, the need is not to propose yet another specific answer, but rather to provide a set of beliefs which are the essential elements over which the debate is about. When attention is drawn to the basic underlying belief structure, then it is possible to compare the implications of a particular set of beliefs with alternative beliefs. A critical examination of beliefs, not conclusions, is required.

Modern/Post-Modern

If today, the 1990s, is a mere continuation of what was before, then higher education is evolving from the economic and political events of the Modern Era which started with the industrial revolution and the modern democratic state. However, if the 1990s are the beginning of the Post-Modern era, which is marked by a new social, economic and political reality, then higher education is more connected with an unknown future than a known past.

A Modern view is much more definite; it is linked to such notions as liberal politics, morality, liberal education, diversity and tolerance, and student services. It is rooted in the belief that there is now great wealth, wisdom and resources at our finger tips, and finally, the technological capacity to deliver their fruits for a new world order. It is the achievement of the modern, democratic, liberal state in which human needs are satisfied, either through extensions of welfare or voluntarism, as humankind harnesses the capacity to live together in a global village. It requires mature, sensitive minds who understand our human history in a way that allows us to capture our destiny from our past. Many within higher education believe this to be true.

A Post-Modern view is much more indefinite; it is linked to such notions as New Era, practical, economic, living and learning, immediate and new activities. Because humankind has the primary task of claiming an unknowable future, there cannot be certainty. Statements about what is "right" or "correct" or "best" are inappropriate. A New Era is marked by experimentation and new activities, existing side-by-side, often incompatible in their philosophical or logical assumptions and purpose, but similar in their tentative, probing nature. They are immediate and practical expressions of the faith that from today's actions will come the coherent form of a future largely unknowable from the past — a past which has fewer and fewer transferable lessons to teach.

Education/Training

This is a dimension which the higher education establishment has created to maintain a distinction between *education* (which is the noblest level of learning because it develops the mind and spirit, much like a fitness centre develops the body, and is reserved for traditional four-year colleges and universities), and *training* (which is a lower form of learning and reserved for technical or specialized schools which do an important but less noble job). Of course they share similarities; both are forms of learning, and both require teaching. Some have suggested that the distinction was dangerous and should never have been made in concept or practice, because each is the most direct and efficient road to the other (e.g., Illich, 1971).

In 1985 the Carnegie Foundation estimated that American business spent an amount of money on training equal to all of what was spent on higher education and had as many learners as were enrolled in all of the four-year colleges and universities (Eurich, 1985). By all accounts the trend noted then has been increasing, both in terms of "in house" education (Wallace, 1990; Eurich, 1991) and in the form of education provided by two-year community colleges (Collison, 1991a; Zwerling, 1988). Industry gives training to compensate for the lack of the knowledge employees need to carry out their work, and which learners seek to be competitive for economic participation. The continuing education that is required to meet the training and re-training needs for national renewal in a New Era has generated a new learning industry.

This new learning industry is a large growth area in what are otherwise difficult economic times. It is remarkable that while the new learning industry is profitable, colleges and universities are struggling. The explanation is in part due to the growing *popular* (not academic) interest in the type of learning I have called "training," relative to the popular disinterest in what I have called "education." The attitudes of students have not escaped attention. Over the past twenty years student interest in college as a preparation for a career has been increasing as shown in Astin's (Astin, et al., 1987) annual survey of college freshmen, reported each year in the January issue of the *Chronicle of Higher Education* (e.g., Astin, 1993). Yet, these attitudes have been the source of considerable faculty dissatisfaction with students found in the Carnegie Foundation (1989) surveys of the professorate.

Moral/Economic

Boyer in his foreword to *Campus Life* (Carnegie Foundation, 1990a) called the 1960s the decade of anger. Then, the anger was over a moral issue. The banner of social justice required trying harder to do what was right. Now, the raw expressions of anger surfacing recently on college campuses are again over diversity (e.g., Magner, 1989; 1990a), but this time they are largely an economic issue over access to power and wealth.

The current debates on campuses on whether regulations which prohibit racially and sexually offensive expressions as a form of harassment (such as a wearing a t-shirt with a red circle and line through the word "homo," or using racial epithets) are infringements on freedom of speech have attracted national attention. *Time* (April 1, 1991) and *Maclean's* (May 27, 1991) have each carried a feature article; and former President Bush, in his commencement address at the University of Michigan, warned that such regulations threaten the flow of ideas and give rise to intolerance, with the Sunday *New York Times* (May 5, 1991) carrying a copy of the text. Faculty groups have formed a national association to oppose what they described as a form of censorship which requires academic content to be "politically correct."

This debate about where to draw the line between enforcing proper etiquette for a scholarly community and infringing on constitutionally-protected freedom of speech and on academic freedom, is distracting from the real issue of the equitable sharing of power and wealth with those excluded: women, the young and minorities. These are the people who the Carnegie Council back in 1980 so clearly warned would be the source of future tension if their legitimate needs were not accommodated. The concerns of the Council are now a reality. The recent conflicts expose the hypocrisy of talking, but not living, the moral imperatives of social justice.

The 1990s are not an unfinished revolution left over from the 1960s. Although diversity is the manifest content, then as now, the current manifestation is new; now the driving force is economics and not what is morally or constitutionally correct. The implications of this issue will be considerable, and it is one that will be examined in detail in Chapter 11, where diversity is explicitly addressed as one of the specific current issues of higher education. The implications of using an economic (not moral) belief as the template will become the central focus of that discussion.

Process

Process issues are concerned with the nature of how change takes place. At an "establishment" level of analysis, which is the focus of this chapter, it is necessary to consider both the structure and the substance of higher education, thus requiring two templates.

Systemic/Institutional

The structure of higher education at an "establishment" level of analysis requires a belief dimension which is parallel to the "person/situation" dimension for the analysis of the academic life of individuals.

There is a "system" or culture of higher education which is captured by national policy and tradition. Similar to an individual's personality, systemic change is usually an evolutionary response to events in the larger social, economic and political context, such as the transition from student populations being majority male to majority female.

But, the system may also change abruptly. The GI Bill, the baby boom and Sputnik combined to transform American higher education in relatively short order. This transformation was imbedded in a larger context that made the developments feel natural. Although less dramatic, we know that the demographics of both the faculty and students will again play a role. For the faculty, a wave of new hiring will start when the faculty of the expansion period start to retire, perhaps rippling into the future with a 40-year period. And, the requirements for life-long learning will change the composition of students and their educational needs. These systemic factors imbedded in the national fabric – similar to gender roles – provide a script which people can live out in a largely unconscious way. The demands seem to arise naturally from the context without any focal point of who or what is the source of the transformation.

In contrast to the system, each institution also has a culture. The decline in popularity of liberal arts colleges has caused them to largely disappear from the landscape (Evangelauf, 1990b), and the Women's College Coalition now counts the number of single sex women's colleges at under 100. The declining student interest in these institutions has caused them to fail or to face an internal challenge of a transformation in character, such as the past debates at Mills (Monaghan, 1990) about whether to become co-educational and at Brandeis (Leatherman, 1990) about preserving its Jewish identity. Large multi-universities have a life of their own which insulates them against such a total institutional identity crisis, but only because of the semi-autonomous units which they have federated together. Any of these units, however, have the capacity to undergo similar transformations of their own, illustrated dramatically by the Department of Education at Boston University taking over responsibility for the nearby Chelsea public school system (Watkins, 1989, 1990a). Sometimes remarkable specific changes can take place when people at a local institution respond to the local manifestations of the "system" in a unique way, relevant for this group of people at this time and place. Many issues of higher education may be seen as institutional, not as just systemic.

Discovery/Adventure

From the standpoint of substance, the process of teaching and learning can be seen primarily as discovery or as adventure; these are two very different processes. Discovery is linked to the past; it is modern and is likely to be system based. The underlying assumption is a philosophy of knowledge that truth and relationships in nature are discovered, forming a body of knowledge which needs to be taught. In the old days – before teaching technology – this was a rote exercise. Today, effective teachers arrange the conditions of experience so that learners can share, in a reconstituted form, the excitement of the original thinker. But, neither the teacher nor the learner is confused; the teacher already knows the answer that the student is to learn. It is an active, engaging form of learning. There is much in life to be discovered, and the less it has to be rote, the more fun for everyone.

In contrast, adventure learning is more like a quest; it is linked to the post-modern and is likely to be institution based. The underlying assumption is a philosophy of knowledge that truth and relationships in nature are "invented," forming a body of knowledge that is socially constructed, the content of which cannot be separated from the process of knowing. Of course, some kinds of knowledge, like the "law" of gravity, are so durable and consistent within our own experience, that they can be treated as if they were discoveries – even though there is no need to think of them as qualitatively different than the socially constructed knowledge of history or of human nature. Effective teaching is opportunistic, capitalizing on events of contemporary importance, for which there are no answers, and to engage students in a process of thinking in which not all will necessarily arrive at the same end point, some of which may be different from the teacher's.

As an example, the Persian Gulf War of 1991 provided a remarkable opportunity for learning which some teachers used to connect academic material with world events (Leatherman, 1991). In a similar way, issues of racial and social diversity have been used to revamp freshman writing courses (e.g., Watkins, 1991). In one of my own classes, the brief existence of the "south-end rapist" raised public awareness and a group of university students turned a class into a learning experience that produced a lasting support service for victims of sexual assault (Renner & Keith, 1985), accomplishing what considerable previous efforts could not (O'Neill & Trickett, 1982). Adventure uses the reality of war, race and gender as not only the occasion, but the reason, for teaching and learning. It is based on a belief that knowledge is not abstract and timeless, but has its truth through expressions in current substance.

Conclusions

Beliefs about higher education fall into three major clusters, having to do with means, ends and processes. This threefold distinction provides the basis for what I have called the Financial Challenge, the Academic Challenge and the Management Challenge. These are three central constructs for a new belief system about the issues of higher education to which we must respond. It is necessary on the one hand to create opportunities out of these three challenges with specific activities that solve the real problems of means, ends and processes. And, on the other hand, it is necessary to have a philosophy for change which responds to each of the three challenges with a coherent and unified set of activities. In short, it will be necessary to be both more specific – as I will be in Section Three – and to be more general – as I will be Section Four – in order to deal with the three substantiative components of higher education.

Section Three
Opportunities

Although 24 beliefs are too many to hold in mind all at once, it is perhaps a surprisingly small number both to explain current problems and to provide useful ways to re-define those issues to turn the three challenges into new opportunities. But, these distinctions are enough to recast current events into new forms with fresh possibilities. This requires pulling together various sub-sets of the beliefs to explain what has happened to produce a particular problem, and what might be done to solve it when the contrasting beliefs are used as templates.

Once a belief is adopted for use, rather than just a private thought, it becomes a template. It becomes a forceful tool for turning events, which in reality flow by in undifferentiated connectedness, into specific "things" (i.e., products of our mind). When people change their beliefs by engaging in what has popularly become known as "re-definition," the new beliefs turn old events into new and different "things." Of course, the events do not actually change; it is the construction of them which changes through re-definition. Beliefs are indeed powerful. When beliefs become templates, they narrow and direct the focus, and dictate and exclude actions as logical and correct, or as irrational and incorrect.

People cannot act without beliefs, which are at least implicit in all actions. When events seem to conspire to trap people into dilemmas which challenge their existence, it is their beliefs which offer the opportunity for escape. In higher education the challenges have presented us with the occasion to re-think what we believe, and in the process, given us the opportunity to re-define events in ways that otherwise would not have been possible.

The beliefs have been arranged into 24 dimensions in order to contrast an old way of thinking with a new way of thinking. Thus, using one variation of the dimension as a template is a way to describe current ways of thinking and the dilemmas they have produced. Using the belief at the other end of the dimension as a template re-defines the issue in a way which creates an escape from the problem. In this section, I will be quite specific, presenting three examples of turning the challenges into opportunities by creating new templates through re-definition. For each of the three challenges, it is a five-step process:

- The first step is to collect the particular **beliefs** which are necessary to construct an explanation of the issue.

- The second step is to collect the necessary **factual** data for a clear local descriptive picture.

- The third step is to "invent" feasible **approaches** through re-definitions which have the potential to be acceptable to all those who have a vested interest and to those who have the power to subvert the initiative.

- The fourth step is to carry the analysis through to the logical conclusion of the practical steps required for **implementation**.

- The fifth step is to put the analysis into a larger **perspective**.

In this section (Section III), the reader is asked to adopt a mindset that is at a "micro" level of analysis. Each chapter contains one specific example of a feasible solution to one of the challenges based on re-definition. The example is not presented as the only answer, but as only one of many possible solutions. Thus, in each chapter, a single substantive "product" is not being promoted for all institutions of higher education, for it will not be universally applicable; but rather, it is the process of similar micro-level, problem-solving re-definitions which may be generalized.

In the following section (Section IV), I will shift to a "macro" level of analysis to consider the general beliefs which are required to bring coherence and direction to the larger process of institutional change that takes place through many specific, micro-level, problem-solving re-definitions.

Chapter 8
The Financial Challenge
Finding the Means

Meeting the financial challenge is only one-third of what must be considered from a simultaneous perspective. Responding to the crisis in higher education neither begins nor ends with the Vice President Finance, although increasingly, academic matters are being driven by budgets, rather than academic values being the basis on which budgets are determined. Academia is upside down. There is more truth than many would care to admit in the suggestion that the Vice President Finance should be an academic, and, with the growing interest in importing business management into academic affairs, that the Vice President Academic should be an accountant. These are signs that it is time to re-examine our beliefs.

Beliefs

In Chapter 2, I suggested that the current financial crisis did not occur without warning, quite independent of the subsequent world-wide economic conditions which have compounded the problem. As was clear in 1980, even without the recession, the financial problems associated with demographic factors alone would have been sufficient to severely challenge the system. Indeed, higher education is not a victim of economic conditions, as both economic structures and higher education are undergoing transformations which can be traced to the common factor of the end of the Modern Era. This larger challenge – the challenge of change – is forcing business, government and education to re-examine the three components of means, ends and processes.

The Old Beliefs

Higher education has been operating on the basis of a set of fundamental beliefs that their problems are general, national and external. This has fixated efforts on getting others to accept responsibility for solutions while those within higher education have remained relatively passive, preferring to argue for a reinstatement of the status quo. This position has resulted in a situation where the problems of higher education are seen as the symptoms resulting from the retrenchment process which is required because of under-funding.

New Beliefs

I have suggested that we adopt the alternative beliefs that the financial challenges facing higher education are not just due to the general economic condition, and they will not right themselves in unison with Wall Street. Quite the contrary. These are the good times for higher education relative to everything else in the world that is "broken" and needs to be "fixed." The financial issue, in particular, is quite **specific**, and therefore requires **internal** adjustments based on **local** actions at individual **institutions**. External and national bodies have neither the means nor good reason to bail out the system (i.e., the Establishment) of higher education. In particular, this includes business, which can solve its immediate training needs much more cheaply and directly through the emerging proprietary sector.

```
          Primary Concepts

Our Circumstances

    General/Specific
    National/Local
    External/Internal

Our Relationships

    Them/Us
    Passive/Active

Means

    Under-funded/Over-extended
    Retrenchment/Dynamism

          Secondary Concepts

Symptoms/Causes
Successive/Simultaneous
Systemic/Institutional
```

Box 8-1: Belief Templates

If new financial resources are to be found, this will require an **active** initiative by the individuals (**us**) at each **institution** to look at the **causes** of why their own resources are **over-extended**. Past exercises of financial restraint based on retrenchment have been cost-ineffective by only reducing the symptom of a yearly short-fall without increasing the capacity to adapt. Future efforts must free resources to create **dynamism**. However, it must be remembered that the issues are not just about means; a financial strategy must be part of a **simultaneous** approach that addresses the full range of issues.

An Illustrative Set of Facts

Problem solving requires information. But "facts" are not nearly as objective as they are often presented as being. Beliefs come first because they selectively direct attention toward particular information and provide the interpretive context. The old beliefs directed attention toward others, the new beliefs toward self.

From the new beliefs, national facts and statistics are not the appropriate level of analysis for problem solving. This is not to deny that national facts are useful for other types of analysis, such as establishing the generality of the local issues as opposed to highly localized problems. Thus, institutions can learn from each other. Each institution needs to collect its own data to have accurate local facts in order to share ownership of the implications of the information with its own university community. Communities are defined by social relationships and by a psychological sense of belonging felt by individuals. Waiting for a common national solution does not create a local sense of community.

Thus, the facts I will present are from a single "typical" university. The facts are illustrative; it is the methodology for creating a local descriptive picture which is general and transferable (for details see Renner, 1986c). Consider first the issue of tenure. As shown in Figure 8-1 on the following page, the faculty is largely tenured. With each round of financial restraint the cuts are most easily applied at the non-tenure track end. Historically, those on a tenure-track are twice as likely than not to be awarded tenure, and those positions where tenure is denied are likely either to be eliminated or converted into limited term or part-time appointments. The net effect is a steady drift from 82% of the full-time faculty lines being locked-in toward the limiting case of 100%.

Most of these individuals are not due to retire until after the year 2000. Then, over an 11 year period, two-thirds of the faculty will reach the nominal retirement age of 65. This locked-in group of faculty are all moving to the top of the salary scale. The financial fact is that the age distribution has been less expensive than an even distribution of ages through 1985. From that date on, however, this age distribution has become progressively more expensive as is shown Figure 8-1. Even if constant salary dollars were available (increases in the salary budget which match inflation), an unlikely condition, it will still be necessary to reduce to the total faculty complement by 15%. Without targeted lay-offs of tenured faculty, such reductions will be by chance and circumstance, not by design.

Further, when departmental budgets are examined, an average of 97% is spent on people. This average amount is deceptively low, because a few departments with expensive laboratories to maintain, such as chemistry and theatre, lower the average. Virtually all money goes to people. Any financial squeeze will increase faculty work load, decrease student services and lower support services. Quality will continue to decline.

There is an absolute mess ahead which will grow progressively worse for at least the next decade. The situation is actually worse for individual institutions than what we are led to believe by national statistics which obscures unique local pictures by averaging out the fact that different institutions expanded at different times and rates (Renner & Mwenifumbo, 1995). Because of the unique local factors, the critical decisions must be made on a campus-by-campus basis by local personnel (e.g., the department of sociology might not have a problem with age distribution at a particular institution even though it is often a problem at other places). Thus, we have a social problem of national dimensions when so many individual institutions are in a similar situation. But social problems manifest themselves in specific places, and solutions have to happen at these places. The new beliefs assert that responsibility for initiation of the solutions should be on the spot, not up the system.

Figure 8-1

Tenure Status of Academic Appointments in the Faculty of Arts and Science

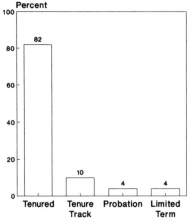

Source: Renner, 1988a

Year of Reaching Age 65 for Tenured Faculty in Arts and Science

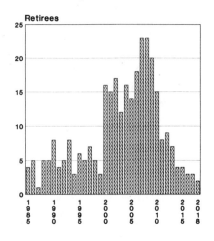

Source: Renner, 1988a

Actual vs Ideal Salary Budgets Faculty of Arts and Science

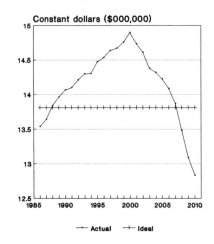

Source: Renner, 1988a

Percentage of Departmental Budget Paid in Salaries

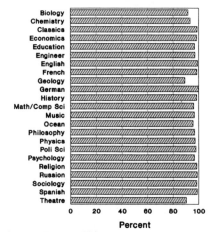

Source: Renner, 1988a

A Feasible Approach

National surveys of faculty in both Canada (Lennards, 1987; Timmons, 1989) and the United States (Carnegie Foundation, 1989; see also, Jacobson, 1985; Mooney, 1989) have shown significant numbers to be unhappy, less energetic and less interested, critical of students, under personal stress and interested in leaving academia. Each institution needs to know this information about all of its own faculty. Again, it is local data that is essential, but lacking. We do not have a national picture that provides a profile of individual institutions rather than a sample of nameless and placeless individuals.

Most faculty, however, feel there is no exit, and they plan to stay for another 10 to 15 years, and rise to the top of the salary scale; and why not? It took hard work and a number of years of deferring income to get to this position. The lifetime earnings of professors are far less than for those with comparable educational levels and competitive screening. Faculty will not and cannot reasonably be expected by others to relinquish this position.

Simple calculations tell us that they are going to cost a great deal of money over the next decade (Renner, 1986c). The question is: *What would be required to provide a genuine alternative in which enough individuals would voluntarily choose to leave?* The answer to determining the necessary social and financial arrangements, the numbers of individuals affected and the net financial saving to be realized are quantitative questions requiring only the use of well developed accounting concepts to provide an answer. The outcome is the means for individuals to increase their own happiness while increased vitality is restored to the university through young replacements hired at less money.

It should be made very clear that this is **not** an early retirement program. Early retirement affects only those individuals who will retire anyway over the next five years; they are not of primary interest. The individuals in question are those who comprise the age bulge that at the illustrative institution are not due to reach age 65 until between the years 2001 and 2010. Many of them, of course, will choose to work longer if they are not required to retire. The target group would be different at other institutions, and Canada will different than the United States where mandatory retirement is no longer in effect.

Implementation

The good news is there is a solution; the bad news is that the ideal time to being such a response was around 1985 when the current faculty started to become more expensive and there was a longer interval both for financial savings and for creating the supply of replacements. Valuable time and resources have been wasted.

Career Alternatives Model

The first requirement is to establish a default set of assumptions in order to be able to calculate the costs and potential savings of inviting the old and expensive to consider a voluntary separation. My model (Renner, 1986a) first calculates the salary that would be paid to each person from the current date to the date of expected retirement (on the average now above the age of 65) using the local pay scale. This is called the *Gross Capital Gain*, reflecting what the university would save if the individual no longer continued in their employment.

Next, the same salary assumptions are used to hire a young replacement at the entry rate and to provide salary increases over the same time period using the same local salary scale; this is called *Replacement Costs*.

A financial incentive, called *Career Alternative Dollars*, is the amount to be offered to individuals who would like out. The default condition in my published model was two months salary for every year of remaining service up to a maximum of 25 years; it was based on the difference between the year 2010 (the last year of the age

Replacement Salary	$30 000	
Replacement Rate	1	
Percentage Increase	0.05	
Inflation Rate	0.05	
Annual Scale Increase	$1 000	
Annual Salary	$60 000	
Years to Retirement	20	
Gross Savings to University	$2 350 891	
Career Alternative Dollars	$200 000	
Cost of Replacement Person	$1 358 913	
Flexibility Dollars for Univ.	$791 979	
Present Worth GROSS Amount		$1 390 000
Present Worth Career Alternative Dollars		$200 000
Present Worth Replacement Costs		$790 000
Present Worth University's Flex Dollars		$400 000

Box 8-2: Forty-Five Year Old

Replacement Salary	$30 000	
Replacement Rate	1	
Percentage Increase	0.05	
Inflation Rate	0.05	
Annual Salary Increase	$1000	
Annual Salary	$75 000	
Years to Retirement	10	
Gross Savings to University	$1 004 985	
Career Alternative Dollars	$125 000	
Cost of Replacement Person	$438 980	
Flexibility Dollars for Univ.	$441 005	
Present Worth GROSS Amount		$795 000
Present Worth Career Alternative Dollars		$125 000
Present Worth Replacement Costs		$345 000
Present Worth University's Flex Dollars		$325 000

Box 8-3: Fifty-Five Year Old

bulge) and the current date at that time, 1985. This value and the formula is, of course, arbitrary; it should reflect the local demography.

The amount left over after the Replacement Costs and Career Alternative Dollars are subtracted from the Gross Capital Gain yields the amount of money saved over the time period and is called financial *Flexibility Dollars*.

Simulations

If only 10% of each age group from the targeted faculty (those due to retire between 2000 and 2010) selected the program, the total savings to the Arts and Science budget would have been over $8.5 million, with a present worth of an immediate windfall of $4 million in 1985 dollars. This financial flexibility is in addition to the capacity to hire an equal number of new faculty to meet new educational demands and responsibilities. The default calculations in my model are based on a 100% replacement policy to ensure that new vitality (dynamism) and not retrenchment is the result of the process.

In terms of 1994 dollars, a 45-year old professor earning $60 000 who could be replace by a new PhD at $30 000 would save the university nearly $800 000 over the time period to the scheduled retirement. And, a 55-year old earning $75 000 per year would save $441 000 over the time period. This information is summarized in Box 8-2 and Box 8-3. The present cash value of the savings is $400 000 in the first case and $325 000 in the second case. The actual values of each variable in the model can be changed to calculate a variety of "what if" scenarios.

Unique calculations, of course, would have to made for the salary scale at each institution, and the simulation would have to be based on the actual salary and age distribution at that institution. Of particular interest are the range of descriptive pictures that emerge under various "what if" scenarios, such as delaying each replacement by one year; this of course reduces replacement costs and provides an up-front loading of the amount of Flexibility Dollars available.

Career Alternatives Cafeteria

The goal for the Career Alternative Dollars is to provide as much subjective value for the money and as little tax bite as possible. My suggestion is to create a career alternatives cafeteria (Renner 1986b) in which the Career Alternative Dollars could be used in any way. For many individuals this involves a variety of inexpensive associations with the university, of benefit to both, which eases the transition from Professor to some alternative lifestyle.

For example, as more and more faculty are forming associations with business (even including philosophy professors on such things as ethics, not just accountants and engineers), there is an interest in retaining access to such things as the university mainframe. When provided on an actual or incremental cost basis, relatively little money provides resources of large subjective value (Renner, 1988a). The model is based on simple utility theory to maximize mutual benefits by making as little money as possible provide what dissatisfied individuals need in order to have a viable and attractive choice, expressed as a genuine preference to get out of an occupation that is stressful to them but has 10 or more years as the minimum sentence.

The current form of the cafeteria I created is an interactive computer program which allows an individual to arrange his or her options in an infinite variety of patterns, and then evaluate them under any specific "what if" conditions. At the end of every computer run the individual gets a printout of the assumptions and financial state of their life under each scenario they create. They can come back with new figures and new options and try a new variation.

At the end of each run it is possible to ask the individual how they feel about that outcome; most people can tell you. There is no pattern to the choices and options selected. There are as many plans as there are individual dreams that people wish to reach for; or, they are motivated to escape from an equally varied set of life's conditions and circumstances that are draining them of energy and joy, some of which are personal but many of which have to do with academic life.

The typical pattern is to spend more time talking with a person about the quality of their life than is actually spent at the computer terminal. There are many among faculty ranks who are no longer thriving, and they want so much to do so, once again. At the same time, there is a backlog of the young, women and minorities waiting to get in, feeling denied, who believe they would thrive if the opportunity were only there. It is time to start moving some pieces. The Modern Era is over, with fewer significant parts for those who have been its principal players these many years.

Perspective

As with each of the challenges, it is necessary to look at them in two different contexts: an immediate practical one, and one in light of a larger picture.

The "Do Nothing" Alternative

No solution will be without its problems and difficulties. Some of the most obvious ones have to do with cash flow, loss of essential talent and insulation of the savings. There is no absolute or general answer to these issues. There are, however, very explicit and inexpensive ways to collect relevant local information on which decisions can be based, and to develop in advance the principles under which the information will be collected and used. People know what is required for them to feel secure, and they can state these requirements (Renner, 1988a).

Consider the issue of cash flow. Because a Career Alternatives program will pay for itself, the only additional cost is the carrying charges on the cash needed to begin the process. It is pointless to speculate on these cash flow needs in the absence of data about the types of career alternatives that will be selected. For tax purposes, most people will spread their Career Alternative Dollars over a variety of options which do not incur real costs until some time in the future.

The actual cash needs can be calculated once a number of individuals, who think they may be interested, use the cafeteria to make the career alternative choices appropriate to them. When this empirical data is summed over a sample of cases, reasonable cost estimates can be made and a variety of possible funding strategies are available (Renner, 1988a), such as a one-time infusion of capital by government or other sources to prime the pump. If it were locally acceptable to delay replacements for one year the process is immediately self-financing and does not require any external support. Although no administration should ask its faculty to delay appointments, the faculty might choose to do so under an appropriate set of circumstances. I will return to this point in Chapter 12.

The issue of who and how many faculty will be attracted to the program needs to be determined. The level of dissatisfaction within academe and the experience with the British early retirement plan (Simpson, 1985) suggest there will not be a shortage of takers. Who they will be is less clear, although recent data (Carnegie Foundation, 1990b; Renner, 1991) is consistent with the older evidence (Patton, 1983) from the faculty development period (AAHE, 1983) that they will be the disaffected. We should not, however, seek or expect a national answer to this question. The answer will vary from institution to institution, and will not be discipline specific; a psychology department at one place may be hell, and at another heaven. The critical data is local, not national, and it is easy to obtain (Renner, 1991).

There is no one correct way to implement a career alternatives program. The number of possible organizational approaches are probably as varied as there are local traditions. Academic bodies, such as the Faculty Senate, are far better suited for the philosophical and policy discussions required to establish the procedural principles which will ensure fairness and protect individual rights, than they are to try to set priorities for vertical cuts. The former is a true example of the "empowerment" required for Total Quality, and the latter, although it involves decision making, is the exact opposite – i.e., "dis-empowerment." A choice between being shot or hanged is no real choice at all. Where collective agreements exist they are probably an excellent mechanism for establishing a fair program to the mutual benefit of the institution, the individual faculty who would voluntarily choose to leave if they could and the faculty who remain.

The bottom line, however, is the question: Are these practical problems worse than the doing nothing? The action taken and the problems so created are after all local, specific and internal, the conditions necessary for actively assuming responsibility and restoring choices between acceptable alternatives.

Means, Ends and Processes

The toughest issue is not any of the practical problems from above; there are many feasible solutions to each one. The issue is whether there can be any assurance that, even with financial flexibility, fundamental problems would be solved. After all, if the status quo is the problem, and if the status quo spends the new financial flexibility, it has the potential to be a short-lived windfall, like the experience in the United Kingdom, in which the early retirement option dissipated its presumed benefits in a few years to return to more of the same financial restraints (Association of Commonwealth Universities, 1985; Taylor-Russell, 1986).

The UK effort, or any effort, that simply produces a brief period of relief is not sufficient. The early retirement effort was a short-term fix of a financial symptom, rather than a coordinated strategy for addressing a fundamental (causal) problem. To spend any money to buy momentary flexibility, as did the British, when flexibility would have occurred anyway over the critical period, is simply wasteful. What is required are responses directed at the fundamental structural problems created by the faculty age distribution, not at the resulting symptom of the yearly budget crisis.

Thus, in addition to the means, there must be compatible micro-level, problem-solving approaches for simultaneously dealing with both the ends and the process. Money is only one part of a three-part puzzle. When all three parts are in hand, it will be possible to address the larger substantive issues of higher education and the general process change. This higher-order material from a macro perspective is in Section Four.

Chapter 9
The Academic Challenge
Defining the Ends

Although the focus is different, the steps are the same: Collect a set of beliefs, create a solution based on facts, devise and evaluate a practical tool for implementation and put the approach in perspective.

The academic challenge is large given the responsibility to assume new educational roles in light of faculty demographics and limited financial flexibility. Meeting the academic challenge will require reallocating flexibility from the future to the present. Borrowed academic flexibility is similar to a non-renewable resource; it must be invested in securing the future, not in reinstating the past.

Beliefs

When the Carnegie Council (1980) used the term "dynamism" they were not talking about somewhere over the rainbow. Dynamism is not the last line of the familiar fairy tale, "and they lived happily ever after." It is about a positive circle based on cooperation that is the opposite of retrenchment. Each change which is made increases the capacity to survive, putting back more than is taken out. A positive cycle is based on the same principles as a negative one, but opposite in its effect. It is absolutely imperative to think this way; there is not enough recoverable financial flexibility to do it all, there is only enough to start a growth process to reach for new ends.

The Old Beliefs

Future gazing is never easy; it is constrained by current beliefs which define what is the obvious and immediate reality. Such beliefs are anchored to the past and only tenuously connected with the future. We can understand the current challenges as symptoms that result from the negative cycle of retrenchment generated by our current beliefs. Primary change threatens the status quo and self-interest will be ready to manifest itself at every opportunity, provoking coercive, not constructive, choices. Such is human nature. The challenge is to stop looking for alternatives which deny these realities, but rather ones which accept them and conspire to contain them.

New Beliefs

It is difficult to think of such a dynamic process when our literal and linear Western minds want to know what the outcome will be, or more likely, what it *should* be. Change is a process, and when it is **primary**, by its very definition it is an **adventure** in which the end cannot be known in advance of the journey itself.

For those who are uncomfortable with holding the belief that these are epochal times, it is sufficient for the current discussion to take a view similar to what Kuhn (1970) proposed for scientific progress. We are at a point when the world of ideas must undergo a paradigm shift. The academic challenge is about **institutional** change. There are two dimensions to this **revolution**, one having to do with the replacement of one set of academic areas of specialization by new ones – literally a new set of substance. The other dimension is the replacement of an internal competitive structure with one which is inter-disciplinary, and builds and encourages **cooperation** and inter-dependencies.

Reaching for the future is an **active, social process** which is directed at correcting fundamental **causes**. We cannot continue to treat the symptoms of academic floundering through endless curriculum debates driven by self-interest, and wait for everything to be all right in the end (which for higher education requires waiting until after the year 2000 for significant change to start). Surely, we can not expect to do problem solving on ourselves (**us**) without the effort of soul searching. This requires taking a **specific**, **local** and **internal** perspective and a **simultaneous** consideration of Ends in the context of Means and Processes.

Primary Concepts
Our Circumstances
General/**Specific**
National/**Local**
External/**Internal**
Our Relationships
Them/**Us**
Passive/**Active**
Our Problems
Technical/**Social**
Product/**Process**
Symptoms/**Causes**
Organizational Change
Secondary/**Primary**
Successive/**Simultaneous**
The World of Ideas
Reform/**Revolution**
Competition/**Cooperation**
Process
Systemic/**Institutional**
Discovery/**Adventure**
Secondary Concept
Coercive/**Constructive**

Box 9-1: Belief Templates

A Feasible Approach

I approached the issue of academic flexibility by asking first, what are the facts? Descriptively, where are we now, and prescriptively, where should we be going? However, I could not find any existing way to meaningfully describe these issues, so I developed an approach which I have called Position Description Analysis (Renner & Skibbens, 1990). The approach is a process which gives the specific factual information needed locally in order to address the issue of the academic ends. The collection of the factual information is itself the approach for addressing the academic challenge. The end can not be known in advance, because the solution is something we do; it is not a uniform national product or one that someone else with great wisdom knows but that the people at a specific institution have not yet discovered.

A Catalog of Knowledge

The first step was to create a catalog of everything that is now done or could be done within a university, regardless of whether or not it is a good idea to do so at any particular university. The purpose of the catalog was to be able to clearly differentiate the current roles and functions of a university, and those towards which it might aspire. Although formidable, the task is not impossible. Libraries do, after all, put a number on each book and place them in a logical order on a shelf. Our granting agencies divide research proposals into major areas on the basis of shared characteristics and send them to even more specialized panels to be evaluated. Our professional associations divide themselves into interest groups which bring like-minded people into the same room at their annual meetings. Our published abstracts organize research into categories which allow us to find similar material. Although none of these reflect the "true" hierarchy of knowledge, and all are open systems in a constant state of change, they all work well enough to satisfy the immediate needs for which they were created.

The catalog we developed used a four-level system. The specializations of knowledge was first divided into 38 areas, with each of these divided into a finite number of fields, and each of these into divisions. Each of these three levels was represented by a two digit number. In addition, each division could be given a speciality subdivision label, also represented by a two digit number. Thus, a potential four tier "tree" was created, in which any area of knowledge could be identified by a unique 8-digit code number. Details of the procedure can be found in Renner & Skibbens (1990).

The Ideal

The catalog can then be used to describe how the existing number of faculty positions ideally should be distributed over the descriptive categories for each department. The ideal distribution was to reflect a department that would capture "emerging areas of specialization, minimize appointments in dying areas, and would generally make the department relevant for the period from the present to the year 2000." Obviously, other definitions are possible, depending on which of its many purposes the tool is being used.

The Actual

A second independent step is to classify the various specializations of all of the existing members of the faculty using the catalog. Some faculty members fit into a single category; others required multiple categories to cover their diverse teaching and research specializations. This process provided a descriptive inventory of the actual faculty resources which allowed each person to be proportioned into as many as three different descriptive code numbers.

The Differences

A large spread sheet underlies Position Description Analysis. The rows are the coded categories of knowledge from the catalog. The major column headings each represent a department and each is composed of three sub-columns: (1) the actual number of FTEs (Full-Time Equivalents) for each code, (2) the ideal numbers of FTEs for each code and (3) the difference between them, obtained by subtracting the ideal from the actual. The actual and the ideal sets of data, based on a common catalog, measured the degree of similarity between the actual and ideal FTEs in areas of faculty specializations. Thus, a positive difference reflects an excess and a negative difference a shortage in the ideal distribution. The absolute value of these three column totals, summed over all areas of specialization, provided a descriptive summary of each department.

When all of the departmental cells are combined into a single spread sheet, in which each row is identified by a unique eight digit number representing an area of either an actual or ideal specialization. The total for each row is the sum of all of the FTE values which use the same eight digit code summed over all departments. These marginal totals provided a picture of the faculty as a whole by identifying the absolute amounts of over- and under-subscription for each category of specialization, regardless of departmental affiliation.

Within a department, the absolute differences will reflect the sum of the excess and the shortage of particular specializations. However, across the faculty, wherever one department has a surplus in an area where another department has a shortage, these differences offset each other, indicating areas for potential departmental cooperation. Thus, the discrepancies within the total faculty are less than the sum of the discrepancies within departments.

An Illustrative Set of Facts

I developed the catalog on the Arts and Science Faculty at one university (Renner & Skibbens, 1990). Thus, the results which follow illustrate the development of the methodology of Position Description Analysis and the type of facts that result. Data on the specific nature of any particular university must, of necessity, arise from a conscious commitment by that university to develop an internal self-description. Otherwise the information can only reflect an unofficial illustrative picture provided by willing research subjects, as is the case here.

Over- and Under-Subscribed

In all, 351.17 FTEs were cataloged, with each current faculty member described by up to three 8-digit code numbers. The same number of FTEs were allocated to an ideal distribution. The sum of the positive differences between the two distributions of FTEs (Actual - Ideal) was 85.405 FTEs. Thus, 24.3% of the faculty provide skills in excess of ideal needs. Or, stated alternatively, the sum of the negative differences indicated that 24.3% of needed roles and functions are not filled. This data is probably a conservative estimate of the degree of under- and over-subscription from the ideal because of the unwillingness of some of our respondents to acknowledge or emphasize discrepancies between the two distributions.

Convergence and Cooperation

Of the total of 475 codes used to catalog the faculty, 82.7% were unique entries used by a single department; often more than one individual fit the category. The remaining 17.3% represented the use of the same code by different departments. As an example, an identical graphics code emerged in three departments. An examination of the course catalog showed that each of these professors taught an undergraduate graphics course and the registration figures showed that each of these classes had a small enrollment. The potential exists in such cases for cross-listing and for more creative use of the freed faculty time, or a gain in flexibility of one-third of the faculty line should one of those positions become vacant.

Implementation

There is no single way to use the approach. It does not matter if each institution changes or adapts the catalog to suit local purposes. Concern over uniformity would only be proposed by someone who believed that a national sample and exact comparative institutional data was important, even if each institution did not like the catalog in some particular, but different, way. It is a perverted sense of what is "legitimate" knowledge that insists that we only deal with that part of reality which is common to a uniform method, rather than allowing the methods to be flexible enough to match the reality that particular institutions may wish to understand. Of course, if my personal purpose was to publish a comparative research study, I would have to insist that each institution comply. In the end, I would have a "product" that no one owned. However, as a problem-solving approach, it is local ownership of the facts which is essential, and it is the process which is general. I have reversed the usual relationship between method and results which is an application of the product/process template.

Constraints

The rules we used for creating the ideal distribution were open-ended. In actual use, institutional constraints need to be defined in advance. For example, if a particular university had made a commitment to adult education and life-long learning this would impose specific obligations on departments and thus set additional constraints on the nature of their ideal distributions. Clearly, a review process is required at each higher level to insure that the roles identified as ideal are consistent with institutional goals and do not simply extend self-justifications of the status quo.

The most important considerations are the demographic and social constraints that each particular institution will face. If the reality of an urban university is that it is going to change from majority white to majority minority, then that must become a constraint. In contrast, if a well-established fraternity and sorority system will ensure a competitive advantage of a particular institution to attract well-off traditional-aged students, then this is an institutional specific fact. For some, such as the recent debate at Mills College over remaining a woman's institution or going co-educational, this will cause an existential crisis; but, at least the debate can be focused.

Academic Values

The ascendency of academic values over accounting values is essential. The power of Position Description Analysis is the fact that different individuals will provide different ideal distributions of FTEs. This is a problem only to someone who confuses reliability with validity. There is no true ideal, only the visions of individual people as members of organizational units. The tool of Position Description Analysis is one means – a process – to articulate their vision with a shared vocabulary. It will allow internal debate, an institutional review system, and a ledger of roles and functions. This, by definition, is a time-consuming political effort, but one with the clear function of directing change as an analytical process, independent of specific personnel decisions. Currently, faculty replacement discussion typically take place in an ad hoc fashion when a position becomes empty without a conceptual balance sheet of specific needs and capacities.

For illustrative purposes, the ideal distribution was based on the same total number of FTEs as actually existed. Although such a balanced ledger may not be a realistic possibility in practice, it is a useful procedure for analytical purposes. Arguments about increases in the required total number of FTEs to reach an ideal raises competitive issues of power and self-justification which, while they cannot be avoided, can be separated from the analytical task of conceptualizing roles and functions. For example, the rationalization for the extra FTEs and the distribution of them over and above the already identified ideal categories can be collected as a separate step, but only after the current number is allocated according to the instructions.

Academic Budgets

The ultimate goal is to have academic decisions drive the budget process. The reverse happens in times of retrenchment when non-replacements are often dictated by chance and circumstance to correct a financial deficit situation. The focus on roles and functions as the *conceptual* units for the university is a shift from the implicit current focus on departments and programs as structural units. By attaching actual budget dollars to the roles and functions of needed or under-subscribed descriptions, rather than to the structural units which administer them, there is a built-in incentive for structural units to embrace inter-disciplinary programs and emerging fields, while disassociating themselves from over-subscribed ones.

While it may be theoretically possible to eliminate all departments and to re-structure the university in terms of roles and functions, it is neither a very likely event nor one that would have probable success. Those with existing structural power would use their position to block the process or to create new structures which accomplished the same ends. A simpler route may be to modify the currency of exchange available to structural units by beginning to link budgets with academic values through the tool of Position Description Analysis.

Perspective

Again, it is necessary to consider practical here-and-now issues as well as the larger picture. A unique feature of Position Description Analysis is that it immediately and personally involves everyone at the university, at least to the degree of calling them an eight digit name. This involuntary nature of the involvement with the process is also a means for achieving commitment. If we must be that heavy-handed, and I think we must for there cannot be individual bystanders, then the process should be one that pulls all, voluntarily or not, into a constructive process.

The "Do Nothing" Alternative

Problematic expressions of self-interest will of course be present with Position Description Analysis, just as they are now, attempting to distort the Ideal picture. The choice, however, is not over whether self-interest is or is not present, but how it will be expressed and how it is best recognized for what it is.

In fact, all of the illustrative data above should be regarded as a conservative estimate of the depth of the problem. Subjects could see the implicit spread sheet and their tendency was to let their current reality, the one that will need to be defended at some point in the future, also be their ideal. But, my developmental work had no review process to help to contain this form of self-interest, nor did it include several "what if" ideals to shift the focus of the exercise to other choices, nor did it have the security built-in to the process which is necessary for individuals to risk foregoing a coercive for a constructive choice.

Position Description Analysis is an open process in which information is created to guide decision making that is aimed toward the future. The purpose of the tool is to allow each unit to create a vision of what it would become if the retrenchment cycle could be broken. As such, the tool must be seen as only one element in a larger policy strategy for higher education which includes the generation of financial flexibility through means other than retrenchment. Once there is means, then and only then, is it possible to envision new ends.

Creating a new vision will require the courage to begin the process of change, although to do so will not be easy. The alternative, however, is to settle for the bottom line of externally imposed solutions, an outcome which is neither in the best interests of individual faculty members nor the university as a whole.

Means, Ends and Processes

Only by providing individuals with security and new opportunities (such as the opportunity for those who want out to have a Career Alternative), and by providing departments with the freedom and safety to be less than the ideal (i.e., to identify roles and functions which are no longer needed and new ones which are needed) can we create the conditions for optimism and change. Both a "means" and an "end" are required to replace the destructive effects of retrenchment with dynamism. No department will identify any area as "over-subscribed" unless it is first safe, and second wise, to do so.

I will return to the importance of this issue, which Deming called "freedom from fear," in Chapter 12 on the social and psychological conditions necessary for implementing change. For now, it is absolutely essential to be unequivocally clear that Position Description Analysis is not an audit tool for creating a hit list, because if PDA is used in that way the essential information will be withheld. If the reader has any thoughts that the tool should serve this purpose it runs contrary to what I am trying to accomplish. The approaches I am illustrating are not part of a retrenchment strategy; they are about creating dynamism.

Socially, as an institution, individual universities must stop asking their members to establish priorities over which programs are more important than others, when the end point is to then sacrifice them. Our efforts to do so sets our organizational units, usually departments, at each other's throats as self-justifications increasingly replace problem solving. Families do not have such discussions, nor are the discussions in any way compatible with the calls for a new sense of "community." Solutions require simultaneous consideration of related issues. We must replace our competitive institutional structures with cooperative ones, and abolish competitive priorities between units. Each unit must be free to invest the flexibility it can generate – its own flexibility – into becoming its own ideal. Every corner of the campus must be able to look toward the future. The crisis in higher education is largely about creating the psychological and social capacity to act (Renner, 1988b) in constructive (not coercive) ways.

Chapter 10
The Management Challenge
Starting the Process

The approach described in this chapter, similar to the ones in the previous two chapters, is a specific action that can be started immediately. It illustrates one way of thinking that starts the process of change. Short of a magic wand, no single approach can meet all aspects of the management challenge. The illustration in this chapter focuses on the specific issue of responding to the need for gaining financial and academic flexibility through the use of the Career Alternatives Model and Position Description Analysis. As such it continues the previous examples and is an illustration of the importance of **simultaneous** problem solving, not successive actions.

In a larger sense, the management challenge is to reduce the amount of destructive internal conflict exemplified by budget wars, to enlist cooperation between and among the various constituencies of the academic community, and to restore the level of morale that comes from individuals sharing common purpose. It is in this sense that the problems and issues of higher education are social and psychological in nature; technical solutions alone – such as the specific approaches in this section – are not enough. These larger issues require global ways of thinking which are developed in the next section where the abstractions can be anchored in the concrete examples provided by the three approaches to the issues of means, ends and processes provided in this section.

Beliefs

Human reactions to tough times – such as those now taking place in higher education – are well understood. There is no point in pleading for greater tolerance, cooperation and self-sacrifice; that will not work. Those are the human behaviors that people reserve for their "family," for those with whom they are connected and inter-dependent. If an administrator has to ask for them, then the necessary conditions are absent. The management challenge is the creation of a new form of community.

The Old Beliefs

The persistent response of retrenchment to attenuate the symptoms of financial restraint has done nothing to fix the fundamental problems; at best it has bought time, and at worst it has compounded problems through increased competition and self-interest. It is pointless to ask or compel a person to do things they are either unable or unwilling to do if the goal is to enlist cooperation and voluntary interdependence.

New Beliefs

There is no short cut to identifying the **causes** and to repairing the damage that has been done. This is an **active** interpersonal process requiring a willingness to put relationships first, before practical problem solving even starts. This requires leadership that understands and accepts some of the important lessons to be learned from Total Quality Management and from feminism. Leaders are increasingly required to become **agents of change** who initiate processes rather than managers who create and administer conclusions.

The best solutions in the world are useless if they are not **acceptable**. The way to find out if something is acceptable is to ask. And if it is not, to ask the follow-up question of what would be acceptable. This is an **internal process**, and it needs to pre-empt the effort to promote any particular solution at any particular institution.

It is also important to remember that social issues which seem pervasive, general and intractable have **local** manifestations; they are not faceless. A problem only exists in actual **institutional** settings where identifiable people act in **specific** ways. Further, it is those local situations which have the maximum amount of **social** influence over individual behaviors. Solutions must stay within human capacity; the **situation** is frequently more malleable than the person, for it provides the context which constrains or sustains individual reactions and choices.

```
Primary Concepts

Our Circumstances

    General/Specific
    National/Local
    External/Internal

Our Relationships

    Them/Us
    Passive/Active

Our Problems

    Technical/Social
    Product/Process
    Symptoms/Causes

Process

    Systemic/Institutional

            Secondary Concepts

    Feasible/Acceptable
    Successive/Simultaneous
    Person/Situation
    Manager of Change/Agent of Change
```

Box 10-1: Belief Templates

Illustrative Facts

The assessment movement in particular has provided some very good tools for asking simple but important questions about the current conditions in higher education. This is especially true for assessing faculty and student attitudes and values, and documenting the important features of the teaching and learning process (see e.g., Menges & Svinicki, 1991).

The Carnegie Survey of Faculty Attitudes

In 1969, 1975, 1984 and again in 1989, the Carnegie Foundation carried out a large-scale national survey of the beliefs, attitudes and values of the professorate in U.S. colleges and universities. The individual questions and the simple descriptive information from the two recent surveys was reported in the *Chronicle of Higher Education* (Jacobson, 1985; Mooney, 1989) and the trends reported in a separate publication by the Carnegie Foundation (1989).

There are some striking features in this data. In 1984, nearly 40 percent of the faculty said they would consider leaving academia. This was at the time of an effort to restore sagging morale and a static closed system by renewal through faculty development (e.g., AAHE Task Force, 1983; Eble & McKeachie, 1985). By the end of the past decade there was no difference in the numbers who wished to leave academia. While the marginally better economic conditions of 1989 and the impact of the vitality efforts may have slightly reduced the level of professional dissatisfaction with the academic profession, the gain was off-set by increasing levels of personal stress and a deteriorating campus environment.

The bottom line, before the effects of the recession and budget cut-backs of the early 1990s, was that there was a significant number of deeply unhappy faculty. For example:

*   44% report their job a source of personal strain
*   20% feel trapped in their profession
*   43% would exercise an early retirement option if offered
*   24% seriously considered a permanent departure in the past two years
*   50% rate the quality of life at their institution as fair or poor
*   63% rate the sense of community at their institution as fair or poor

Life in academe is not always easy; by its competitive nature, many are denied the public rewards and acknowledgements of success, and the private ones, the joys of having a significant impact on particular students, are invisible to others and minimally rewarded (Astin, et al., 1991; Boyer, 1990). There are enough people marking time, who typically have 10 to 20 years to go before retirement, to gain the needed flexibility.

The Canadian Survey

In Canada, there has been a similar national survey of the professorate (Lennards, 1987) which asked many of the same questions as the Carnegie survey in the United States, as well as some specific to Canada, such as the penetration of American values. The Canadian faculty are, relatively speaking, less dissatisfied; but, Canada never expanded access at the same rate as the

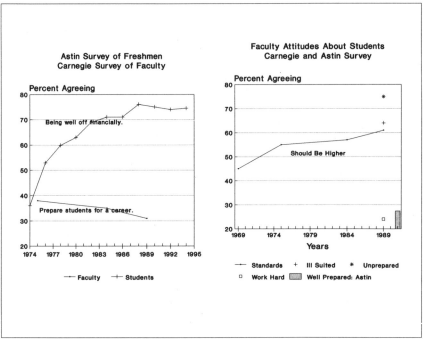

Figure 10-1: Faculty and Student Attitudes

United States (Anisef & Okihiro, 1982), allowing room for off-setting the demographic depression short of the intense registration wars that are becoming commonplace in the United States (Wilson, 1990a, 1990b).

But, in Canada, as well as in the United States, there has been a restricted academic work force, retrenchment and dissatisfaction among a significant number of the professorate (Lennards, 1987):

- 60% say over the past five years morale has become worse

- 26% say morale is generally high

- 36% find their work a source of considerable personal strain

- 32% would not hesitate to leave academic life

- 33% are no longer as enthusiastic about their work as they use to be

Astin's Annual Survey of Freshmen

Each year the Higher Education Research Institute at the University of California conducts a national survey of freshman attitudes, beliefs and values. The results are reported each January in the *Chronicle of Higher Education* (e.g., Astin, 1993) and 20-year trends have been published (Astin, et al., 1987).

Thus, the second part of the teaching/learning relationship has also been well described, if not well understood. A comparison of the beliefs of the twenty-something generation (Astin, et al., 1987) with those of the faculty (Astin, et al., 1991; Carnegie Foundation, 1989) is like two ships passing in the night as illustrated in Figure 10-1. For example:

- 75% of freshmen give as the principal reason for attending college is to get a better job and for being well-off financially, while faculty interest in preparing students for a career has declined over the years.

- over half of the students believe themselves to be above average in academic ability while most faculty see them as unprepared, ill-suited and unwilling to work hard.

There are increasing levels of dissatisfaction among the faculty with the students, their level of preparedness, their work habits, and their attitudes and motivation regarding higher education. Paradoxically, the grade inflation and the recruitment of a wider range of students that universities used as the mechanism to reduce the economic pressure that contributed to faculty dissatisfaction in the first place, has now become an added component to their dissatisfaction.

The growing distance and lack of communication will only grow larger throughout this decade as the age, gender and race gap continues to widen. There is a New Era of students being served by a system designed, manned and managed by the vision of adult people of the 1960s who are now 45 to 55 years old.

Constructive Use of the Information

This kind of survey data provides a useful general picture. Such data helps to frame issues, and because it gets national publicity and can contribute to consciousness raising. But this is not enough, and it can be destructive.

The information is often used for the wrong reasons. The national annual surveys of college freshmen, and the negative evaluations of the findings by faculty members, has resulted in criticism of students. The information, like all socially-constructed knowledge, serves particular and often partisan purposes, such as blaming the primary and secondary schools, and teacher training, as the causes of "the problem." Such attacks may be appropriate if the point is to win a debate over the issue of whether faculty dissatisfaction with *their clients* is to be defined as a problem requiring *others* to change. However, if the students and their public school teachers on the other end are *not* the enemy, and the purpose is to problem solve and improve the relationship, then the use of the information for blaming is destructive.

What we must do instead is turn our energy toward learning why these attitudes exist, how they interact and what can be done to overcome their implications by the specific people who hold them and face each other every day on campuses across the country. Teachers do not uniformly collect this information, yet such data is easy to obtain. One of the primary requirements for total quality improvement is management based on clear descriptive facts.

A Feasible Solution

The focus of these types of surveys needs to be shifted from seeing the results as a product to a general process for gaining the local information required to inform change. The information must describe specific people at a specific place. When this is done, the information is connected to actors who have the capacity to effect changes and to negotiate directly with the sources of their own discomfort. Internal, local and specific are the necessary conditions for individuals to accept responsibility for the solutions to a condition which adversely affects them.

For example, if there are a significant number of faculty at a given place who are no longer happy in nor committed to academic life, then it is in the interests of the institution and both those who are happy and those who are disaffected to find a solution that is to everyone's benefit, such as a career alternative program. The central point is that the "scientific" value of these surveys is not the product of national averages; the only thing that should be generalized is the method. The truly useful knowledge is the local data, which describes a social reality for actual people, that can be used to inform change. National averages are only reference points for social comparison.

The Carnegie Survey

An interest in process questions, rather than a product, requires descriptive information to be used in ways which show relationships between relevant variables. For example, the Carnegie Foundation (1990b) examined the characteristics of those individuals who said they would like to retire early. Significantly more of those who would retire early were less enthusiastic about their career than when they began their career and they endorsed such items as:

- If I had it to do over again, I would not become a college teacher.
- I often wish I had entered another profession.
- My job is the source of considerable personal strain.

The study concluded there was a malaise among the 40% of today's faculty who would like to retire early. They wrote: "Alienated professors are unlikely to be among the effective instructors in academe. Even with early retirement, most will be teaching for another 5 to 25 years." These are the suggestions that should prompt specific local information. What is still not known is how these individuals are distributed across institutions and units within individual colleges and universities.

A Local Application

A one university, for example, 40% said they would be interested in a Career Alternative and 19% felt trapped in their career. These numbers are identical to the Carnegie data but higher than the Canadian average (Renner, 1991). Similar to the Carnegie data, those who expressed an interest in a Career Alternative were also significantly more likely to feel trapped in their profes-

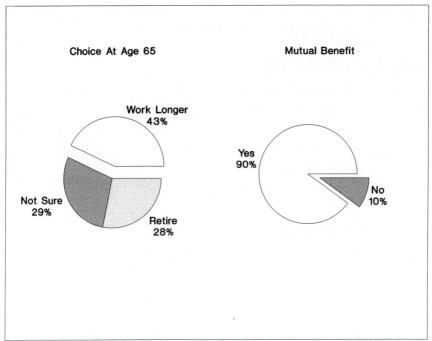

Figure 10-2: Results of Faculty Survey

sion, less enthusiastic about their work than they used to be, and, if they could start again, would be less likely to choose an academic career.

Yet, many will continue to work after the age of 65 (see Figure 10-2) if they are not forced to retire. Professors start earning relatively late in life, and have relatively low lifetime earnings for their educational level. However, the financial cost of providing a desirable alternative can be determined simply by asking. As already described, providing a viable alternative is far less expensive than the cost of keeping them in a job they no longer enjoy simply because there is no acceptable way out. Most of the faculty, including both those who would choose to stay and those who would voluntarily accept a separation arrangement, thought the plan would be of mutual benefit to individuals and to the university.

Because this research was on career alternatives, the subjects were asked additional questions about this issue. Sixty percent of them felt that the institution would use the program to try and force wanted resignations and 44% said they would not trust the administration to develop such a program, with 86% saying it should be incorporated into the collective agreement. It is important to note that this university had two faculty strikes and twice declared a condition of financial constraint. The political reality at this university and at others with serious labor conflicts (Blum, 1990c), are probably similar to each other, but different from many others. Once such local data is in hand, as open public information which is intended to inform change, rather than blame, then the ingredients for problem solving are in place.

Implementation

It is easy to learn the answers to such issues as: What are the characteristics of the people who are dissatisfied here? Would it be of mutual benefit to them and the university to have a career alternatives program? How would we arrange it to be fair? Such information is necessary for the process of a career alternatives program to evolve. However, such information is politically sensitive. Its ownership has the capacity for one-side use (for institutional benefit, not individual or mutual benefit), which has contributed to faculty resistance to such data files, which, in practice, becomes a choice to make important decisions based on ignorance. Concerns over the use of information are legitimate. For example, for Position Description Analysis this information has to be collected in a context in which it is not only safe, but is indeed desirable, to be less than perfect. However, for a college or university to be ill-informed and ill-advised on such matters is without excuse. Yet, on matters most fundamental to the solutions of current problems, uninformed debates are carried out in Senate.

Institutional Research

The office of institutional research usually reports to the President. The information and analysis is often treated as confidential and used for administrative purposes, sometimes as part of the collective bargaining process in ways which are experienced as negative to faculty interests (e.g., reasons why restrictions on tenure should be increased). A more useful function should be factual reports to the campus community and in the maintenance of read-only data files on the university computer system, thus openly encouraging independent analysis and involvement. A Carnegie or Astin type of campus survey, modified to include marker items from the national data set, and other items relevant to specific campus issues – as illustrated above for one university – when put in the public realm, can become the information needed for individual involvement and problem solving. Part of campus life needs to be a detailed description of important attitudes, beliefs and values, and the means to look for relationships between them from more than a one-sided view. It is from the paradox between different versions of the same truth that re-definitions are constructed (Rappaport, 1981). The way to preach an open, inquiring academic community is to live it as well.

Management and Agent of Change

The secret to meeting the management challenge is to lose control over the outcome. For an administration to develop a career alternative program, have it approved by the Board and then present it to the faculty would be to invite conflict. In contrast, to present a structured problem, such as the career alternative model and position description analysis, with complete institutional data, is to invite participation and the creation of something that will have the chance to be both feasible and acceptable. Of course, the project has to be well managed and the data collected must be sound; but, competent administration is not to be confused with management. For example, the entries in the Position Description Catalog must provide a reasonable home for most people, and the information has to be tied to an explicit decision process known in advance. But, these are technical issues for which colleges and universities more than have the necessary skills to create the kind of information required to inform change.

In the information age, the technical aspects of knowing are not a problem; the problem is social understanding of how information is to be used. The danger is in attempts to control the outcome by managing the process in order to achieve a pre-determined solution. A particular solution cannot be the goal; rather, the goal should be the achievement of any one of the many feasible solutions which is also acceptable.

If, as was the case in the example, 90% of the faculty believe that a career alternatives program would benefit individuals and the institution, but most did not trust the administration and 86% felt it should be in the collective agreement, then the data reveals the specific institutional constraints: There is consensus to try. If it needs to be in the collective agreement for people to feel safe, then it is a practical question of whether the responsible individuals in the administration and union can work out the details through negotiation, which, if the goal is for mutual benefit, does not have to be a zero-sum game. Information on what it would take for people to feel secure is useful information for seeking alternative solutions. This is all easy and inexpensive to obtain.

An agent of change does not believe "It is all up to me." She believes that under the proper conditions, with people who are not at cross purposes with each other, a viable solution can be found, from among the many that are probably possible. A policeman and an armed robber, face to face, is a different matter; a family's or campus community's best interest is each other's welfare. Having a particular solution is less important than having a feasible, acceptable solution. People have to be given alternatives to claim an outcome with which they are prepared to live. These issues are *not* largely technical, they are social and psychological in nature.

Levels of "Management"

The discussion is not just for administrators. The management challenge is about a process that is applicable to a wide range of issues from the President's Office down to the classroom of every faculty member. The kind of specific information that is necessary for the implementation of a career alternatives program is also applicable to the gap between individual students and faculty in the specific classrooms that bring them together. Nor are we going to change without a dialog that goes beyond blaming. It is a small step to turn each of our classrooms into a post-modern learning laboratory, where one of the purposes of each class is to inform the teaching and learning process (Cross, 1988; 1990). It only requires respect by both parties to ask of the other, what is the nature of the gap and what can we do about it? It is the difference between telling and listening as problem solving, between product and process thinking. It is a belief that problems are not faceless, and that they have local manifestations in specific situations. The national, general, external, system analysis can help us frame issues and raise awareness, but change takes place with responsible actors in known places. Those actions leave traces, and traces are the forms of knowledge that inform change.

Perspective

One of the most telling commentaries on life today is the contradictions. We say we want integrity, but we do not demand it of our leaders; we say we want people to delay gratification, but we are surrounded by appeals for satisfaction now, through the plastic card; we say we want gender equality, but in commercials we drape attractive women over automobiles; we say we want gentleness, yet we make more violent movies and average eight acts of violence per hour on TV; and the list goes on and on. We praise equality of opportunity and the importance of diversity, yet we do not individually insure that it is achieved. But in fact, what we do is what we actually teach (Elmore, 1989).

The post-modern era is about backing off from preaching timeless truths; it is about linking living and learning through seeking alternative solutions to timeless problems. There are no answers that a few of us possess, and that the rest, through skillful management, need to discover. There is a quest for joint partnerships in seeking information that can inform change. The individuals who understand this can become agents of change, and therein provide leadership.

The "Do Nothing" Alternative

To do nothing different other than what we now do should be the standard of comparison. To continue to seek "real" solutions, e.g., "we need to set some priorities," independent of the human capacity for change, is only to fool ourselves that something is being done. A feasible solution is no solution at all if it is not also acceptable (i.e., within human capacity). The solution to a problem, and then the acceptance of it, cannot be done successively, but only simultaneously. Change is not additive, it is multiplicative; if any necessary element is zero the outcome is null. Moving from a product to a process mind will not be easy; we do not know how to do this well, nor do we have well-developed procedures within academe for the issues of higher education. However, these difficulties are not sufficient for doing nothing different, which is to choose by default for a certain decline.

Means, Ends and Processes

I have only touched on some of the process issues which require organizational and systemic levels of thinking. This is the material of the next section. But, as a general summary, the management challenge is to be sensitive to the perspective that the means and ends themselves are no solution independent of what the principal players are willing and able to do. Administrators cannot manage, e.g., make individuals be cooperative nor actually achieve affirmative action in minority admissions; they can become agents of change enabling these processes to take place. An agent of change assumes responsibility for instituting forceful and sometimes intrusive processes, but not outcomes. A manager wants a mission statement from which to develop strategic plans. The difference between them is needing to know the answer before being able to act (managing change), versus first acting on an unsolved problem by having a process in order to achieve an answer (an agent of change).

As the rate of change continues to increase, the balance between the need for these two forms of management will shift. Evolutionary change can be managed. The revolutionary change implied by paradigm shifts and by massive transformations of roles and functions is achieved by agents of change. Thus, the focus is shifted from technical to social and psychological. Survival of a sense of self (not species or culture) is the time-compressed unit permitting or blocking change and personal survival.

Section Four
Change

Change is an odd mixture of contrary forces and personal reactions. On the one hand, disruptions of the status quo can be threatening and the reaction defensive and the mood depressed, while on the other hand, the creation of something new can be stimulating and the response one of openness and energy. Change is both up and down.

The impetus for change often comes from challenges which threaten the continuation of the present. In this way challenges are also opportunities to re-examine the old and to become part of something new. The future is always supplanting the past; such is the nature of progress. However, when change is primary, as it is for most institutions today, the currency of exchange is not just over the substance of the ideas, but also over who will control them and the organizational machine to put them together. When appropriately harnessed, these three dimensions of change – the substance, the people and the nature of the organization – achieve coherence resulting in consistency of purpose and direction across all elements of the organization. In higher education, these are the elements of the financial, academic and management challenges.

In this section, the new beliefs will be used to introduce global ways of thinking which allows the means, ends and processes to be simultaneous parts of addressing the substance, people and organization of higher education. These are the prescriptive beliefs for assuming academic leadership and becoming an agent of change.

Chapter 11
The Substance
Higher Education Issues

There are two ways to approach the substance of higher education. The first is to apply the general perspective provided by the three concepts of the financial, academic and management challenges to the traditional content-based sub-divisions of the field. This approach emphasizes the inter-dependencies between the substantive areas and might be preferred by a Vice President of Finance or Academic Affairs.

The second way is to reverse the order by taking any of the familiar substantive issues of higher education, such as the curriculum, diversity, cost-containment or community, as an individual focus. This organization of the material emphasizes that any issue has financial, academic and management aspects that must be simultaneously taken into account. A committee on equal opportunity in education might prefer this approach.

It is arbitrary whether the general concepts subsume content or the content subsumes concept. I will do both in this chapter. For either approach, the task will be to use combinations of the new beliefs to re-define the substantive issues of higher education. This is an inventive problem-solving process; it is not one of discovering truth, i.e., the "right" answer. Rather, the purpose is to explore and illustrate the implications of using the new beliefs as the first step for embracing change.

The Challenges

The first approach is the most useful for providing a systems perspective. Thinking of content in terms of the three challenges is integrative and leads most easily toward policy and planning. It serves as a reminder that the means, ends and processes of the higher education must simultaneously come together across the entire substance of higher education, bringing their interdependency into focus.

The Financial Challenge

The process of retrenchment must give way to dynamism. Out-dated equipment must be replaced, the teaching technology upgraded, and deferred maintenance must be attended to; it is either pay now or pay a lot more later. This belief is critical for relinquishing the past and reaching for an as yet undefined future. Supporting the current quality of life by depleting the capacity of the system to sustain itself in the future is no more acceptable for the university than for the environment.

However, unlike the environment, which has no legislated, chartered or certified institutional voice, each university does. Under the old beliefs, institutions experienced an internal dilemma of choosing either self-destruction now or later. These choices have been made knowing full well that the nickels saved to meet each financial crisis are going to cost much more than five cents in the future, although their actual costs will never be shown on a financial ledger. For example, the endless user-pay fees that are being tacked on to all operations deepen alienation and loss of community; when faculty salary increases are directly linked to increases in student tuition, those who most need each other face off instead.

The need for financial flexibility touches every aspect of campus life. If those who must work together play a zero sum game, they will spend their energy fighting, of that we can be sure. Letting the tired and disaffected faculty out is surely a benefit to them and to those who will choose to stay out of desire. The Career Alternatives Model and the academic budgets of Position Description Analysis are examples of activities where all can work together toward a common end.

> Primary Concepts
>
> Our Relationships
>
> > Them/Us
> > Passive/**Active**
>
> Organizational Change
>
> > Secondary/**Primary**
> > Successive/**Simultaneous**
>
> The World of Ideas
>
> > Reform/**Revolution**
> > Competition/**Cooperation**
>
> The Industry of Ideas
>
> > Bureaucratic/**Community**
> > Person/**Situation**
> > Manager of Change/**Agent of Change**
>
> Ends
>
> > Modern/**Post-Modern**
> > Education/**Training**
> > Moral/**Economic**
>
> Process
>
> > Systemic (Establishment)/**Institutional**
> > Discovery/**Adventure**
>
> > Additional Concepts
>
> > Symptom/**Causes**
> > Retrenchment/**Dynamism**

Box 11-1: Belief Templates

The Academic Challenge

Faculty and students need to be kindred spirits, united perhaps in direction, but most certainly in adventure. In a New Era, direction is problematic, because by definition, it cannot be known in advance which of all the possible directions would have been best. However, trying to figure out what we should *all* be doing is far different than all doing what we should – embarking on adventures for which there is a willing and able critical mass.

The "Information Age" is perhaps an unfortunate term because it makes learning sound like an endless and hopeless passive activity. Indeed, there is a sense in which the overwhelming fear that some (particularly those over 25) have of computers is "I can't learn all this."

It is the learning establishment that feeds and profits from the "overwhelmed" myth through the bureaucratic mechanisms of professionalization and credentialization. Although it is increasingly possible to give knowledge away, to make it freely available, we now have more than half the population seeking a credential, rather than what they need and want to know. Meanwhile, the faculty complain in the Carnegie Foundation (1989) surveys that the students are too grade and career centred, and becoming more so. The new beliefs point to the fundamental cause as a more situational result of the learning industry than the nature of the persons in our classrooms. Deming's 15/85 rule for business – workers are responsible for 15% of the problem and the system for the other 85% (Walton, 1986) – is probably accurate for higher education as well.

Although the "Age of Adventure" is less accurate descriptively, it is more open and invitational. It channels the fear arising from uncertainty toward exploration rather than retreat or becoming defensive. Just as Dulciana was drawn into the quest of Don Quixote, unsuspecting and unaware, to be transformed into a new self-respecting person which she could not even imagine before, so too the academic challenge is both an illusion and the future that must become a reality. In the New Era, the standard for the legitimacy of knowledge must become the extent and speed with which it can be instantaneously shared at the lowest possible cost with the largest number of people. Knowledge can no longer be a commodity exchange item; it must become as accessible as a picnic for adult and life-long learners of all social classes and races, to be picked up with the same ease as the fast foods necessary for a spontaneous outing.

Of course, in another sense, there is no denying that we are in the Information Age. The two billion or more dollars being spent in the United States alone on the mapping of the genetic codes is intimidating. Only a relatively few can both grasp and feel excitement about such scientific and technological capacity; they understand full well that the next major moral dilemmas that will face humankind will come from the biological and behavioral science, dwarfing all previous ones by comparison, including life under the mushroom tree. This and similar expensive high technology science reflects the true sense of the information age and the dangers of scientific entrepreneurs treating knowledge as one would real estate or other investments, i.e., knowledge is to be owned and managed by an elite who in exchange for control promise to prevent misuse and to serve the self-defined general welfare.

The university as the home of both knowledge as a commodity and (forgetfully so) as an adventure is caught between these opposing tensions. Paradoxically, serving one is experienced as a dilemma of interfering with the other. But, dilemmas are creations of our beliefs. We do not have to quit modern science in order to also be in the business of mass education. Wider and wider capacity to participate in the new era is essential, a paper credential is not.

The Management Challenge

In higher education, there are too many managers and too many people who are trying to do things right to better manage the system; they have increased at over four times the rate of student growth (Halfond, 1991). True adventures are not made up of managers, they are made up of participants. In adventures there are roles for all, but authority for few. Agents of change do the right thing; they facilitate adventures by arranging circumstances that bring people together in ways that prompt spontaneous activities, arising from the dynamics of the group; activities which are therefore owned by the group and are the responsibility of the group. Leaders emerge, often only for the event itself, and all who participate have a self-claimed role and function.

In contrast, managers of change plan prescribed activities, assign roles and post schedules; but, unless the role of manager has been conferred by the group, rather than been assumed by a position, an adventure is unlikely to be the final outcome. This is a hard lesson. Agents of change do not have nor do they want the power to control; managers do. It is the rare individual who plays both roles and does not get the two processes confused.

Summary

Challenges are collective and inclusive adventures. We must free resources that do not force us to compete against each other, we must respectfully collaborate on mutual academic goals as equal partners, and we must structurally and organizationally arrange ourselves to make this happen. This is not a conceptually difficult task; but, it is extremely difficult as a social and psychological process.

The Curriculum

On the surface, the curriculum debate in higher education appears to be about content, but it is not. Although we know that we need a faculty who no longer have an investment in the status quo (i.e., *their* courses, *their* journals and *their* associations), we ask them to decided what should be taught. Derek Bok (1986) has commented that the fascination with curriculum is "to protect traditional faculty prerogatives at the cost of diverting attention away from the kind of inquiry and discussion that are most likely to improve the process of learning" (p. 70). Yet, we are disturbed and even surprised by the divisive conflict that emerges between the establishment and the academic underclass (i.e., women, the young, minorities and non-traditional) over the role of the classics and a traditional liberal education versus alternative material. The principal value of the underclass is not their gender, age, race or life experiences per se, but rather their lack of reverence for and investment in the past, and their commitment to a future of untried ways and unknown answers.

For most people, curriculum implies a discipline-based sequence of classes appropriate for achieving specific purposes, for example, humanistic engineers and scientifically literate humanitarians. But, the current problem of gaining agreement on what these courses are is the symptom, not the problem. The problems of the curriculum reside in academic structures, roles and functions. Until these more fundamental considerations are addressed, the curriculum debate cannot move forward. This will require using new beliefs to dissolve three traditional boundaries resulting from the old beliefs.

Education/Training Boundaries

The time for education is in fast decline and will soon be over relative to the time and need for training. Higher education continues to separate learning from living at the very time when the rate of social, cultural and technological change makes it even more important than ever to reduce such temporal delays between learning and living.

Education implies learning how to think in order to be able to do. Training implies leaning how to do in order to be able to participate, to belong, and through this process learning to think. Change is happening too fast for learning to be for tomorrow; it must be for now if it is to reach the now generation. The new ethnic mix of students and the full range of ages want to participate, and indeed must know how to do so. Once participation is assured, then reflection is possible. In the past, the reflection provided by a liberal education has been a luxury reserved for those already assured participation through a position of privilege.

The rapid growth of community colleges – to now account for nearly half (43%) of all students attending college and university – relative to four-year institutions reflects a success story that can only continue to grow. It is a story of a wide variety of students paying for highly specific training that allows them to become or remain competitive and to participate economically in life. Many of these continuing learners will go on for education, beyond their training; such is the power of an assured economic position.

The exception to this trend will be educational boutiques where the affluent upper class can mix with their own. Only a few select private schools can afford to compete for this market, as even fewer of the eligible students will choose them, simply because what was once an excellent preparation for life will becoming increasingly less so. More training, less abstract learning is the future direction for most colleges and universities.

The obstacles to making this change are our internal organization and management, budgeting by departments rather than academic roles and functions, and the discipline-based specialized way of life academics have created for themselves. The solution is not to go back to the familiar of what was good for us, but rather to go forward to a New Era. The phrase, "Son, when I was your age . . ." is a contradiction of modern reality. Only a short time ago a father or teacher could say those words, because the elder's reality at that age was not appreciably different than that of his son or student. Wisdom is no longer so strongly correlated with age.

Post-modernism is a new way of life, and appropriately so. For example, increasingly psychotherapy is out because it is too slow; self-help is in because it is direct and focused. A meaningful philosophy of life is a contradiction, because more than one will be required in a lifetime. However, meaningful participation is not; inclusion is first, and it is essential for reflection about what it all means. The action is first, the thoughts are second. Our aboriginal peoples have understood the value of this type of education for generations; it is time for the rest of us to catch up.

Product/Process Boundaries

The growing desire found in the Carnegie Foundation (1989) surveys of faculty for a return to a classical liberal education is an effort to reclaim the past. However, as Ornstein and Ehrlich (1989) have pointed out, science and technology make up at least half of our culture, probably more, yet one-fourth or less of the *Cultural Literacy* by Hirsch (1987) is concerned with science and technology, and much of that irrelevant to our future. Yes, there is a need for engineers to understand philosophy, and philosophers to understand the biological revolution. But, a traditional liberal education is not the path. For both sciences and the humanities, the modern liberal education must be integrated and immediate. It is scholarship which is both philosophy and biology, pure and applied at the same time, simultaneous and not successive in its connection with life.

Courses and programs of study which do this have no shortage of students, in particular, those having to do with peace and the environment, and which combine history, geography, economics and political science (Dodge, 1990, 1991). Literature has been combined with philosophy to analyze contemporary moral issues (Bailey, 1987) and to teach logic through murder mysteries (Mangan, 1989). Many prototypes exist.

Today's students are not lazy or afraid of challenges. At Ohio University, they flock to a course taught by a professional comic writer which requires them to give a stand-up routine in the school pub, with the applause and laughter they generate as their grade (Collison, 1988). Why? Because humor is a part of life, from business to New Era psychotherapy. When I do crisis intervention it is quite common for my client to be laughing and crying at the same time about their situation; therein lies the courage to walk among the ruins of a current event and start to pick up the pieces of their future. Yet, how many business schools or programs in clinical psychology are looking to make a joint appointment with theatre? At one point when I was doing research and training in crisis intervention other psychologists put up signs saying "Quiet – Research Area," totally unable to comprehend the combination of knowledge making, laughter and learning.

In Halifax, the local support service for victims of sexual assault grew out of my community psychology class (Renner & Keith, 1985). It is now an independent community agency in its own physical facility, run by a community board. I trained the first volunteers (who now train those who follow them). The university gave away knowledge, connected caring, living and learning; and, for many of the volunteers, their training became a stepping-stone to come back for traditional education. The initial undertaking became an continuing adventure. Volunteers who were also students documented every case that had been handled by the courts (Yurchesyn, Keith & Renner, 1992). At any one time perhaps 100 people were working on the combination of direct service, public education and social action. There is no line between theory and practice, research and service, or knowing and doing; there are only adventures.

We need to teach in more creative ways. We do not do so because we keep looking at the content of what they should know from the "product" display case. This is not to say that content is unimportant, but rather that there is an additional necessary component or the content never gets learned. The insistence from educational theory of always introducing process into a discussion of learning is often used as a criticism by others as an example of the lack of substance of the field of education, and as an illustration of what is wrong with public schools. However, college teachers suffer just as much from the opposite effect of too much content expertise and far too little capacity to share effectively what they know. Similar to multiplication, the fact is that if either of the elements approach zero, nothing much is the product, but the closer the two are to an equal value, the larger the result.

The craft of creative teaching is no more or less a form of art, nor any more or less mysterious, than any other form of knowledge. The simple step, which is formally labelled as "action-research" in the next chapter, of using the process of teaching to inform what actions lead to what consequences under what conditions is a process identical to what created the content itself. Anyone who can acquire and contribute to knowledge can use the same process to also know and communicate about creative teaching (Cross, 1991; Weimer, 1990). It is the same process that is fundamental to all knowing.

One of the most destructive consequences of retrenchment has been a life-boat mentality of looking for someone to throw overboard. Departments of Education have been the weak sister to kick around every time there is a need to talk of vertical cuts. Because Education represents all of the disciplines, they are vulnerable to be taken over by those with the "real" product (it is mathematics, geography, etc. which are the subject matters to be taught). What education does, however, is combine substance with purpose, values and application – the very integration of scholarship needed for the New Era. Paradoxically, to the extent anyone among us has the capacity to lay the golden egg, it is the very goose that disciplines are about to kill for their own survival.

There could not be a more laudable desire arising from the report *A Nation Prepared* (Task Force on Teaching, 1986) than to save the children. Under the joint sponsorship of the then President of Stanford University (Kennedy, 1987) and the Director of the American Association of Higher Education (Edgerton, 1987, 1988) "partnerships" between America's schools and colleges were formed to develop teaching as a profession (Wilbur & Lambert, 1990). The criticism that these efforts are misplaced and self-serving may seem too harsh because, with the steady decline of the SAT scores (Dodge, 1991b), the importance of reclaiming public education is so obvious. However, rather than a partnership to fix the teachers, the experiment by Boston University to run the Chelsea public schools is far more courageous and right on the mark of recognizing that theory and practice are inextricably linked in life. The "wisdom" of how to fix the problem is not just academic, but includes the reality that schools and School Boards are political entities that can pull the plug on the best of theories (Watkins, 1990a, 1990b).

It is unlikely that fixing teacher training by imposing discipline-based "higher" standards and the professionalization of teaching will solve the problems of primary and secondary education, although it does allocate blame and gives higher education a politically acceptable scapegoat (Burbules & Densmore, 1991). This solution has been picked because it serves the self-interests of the status quo. The real solution is education that is about life. Teachers have always been willing to teach this way; but, they have been stifled by those who look to the past, not the future. It is school boards, parents and even the Pope (Blum, 1990a, 1990b), who keep trying to separate living and learning by declaring some of the most pressing social topics to be unacceptable content for education, such as contraception, abortion, homosexuality and AIDS.

We should stop teacher-bashing and look at how product thinking has taken over the process of education (Edgerton, 1991). The danger is that more and more public colleges and universities will come to resemble the public schools with ever larger investments in their own fixed establishments without sufficient incentive to capture their own future (Zemsky & Massy, 1990). Demographically, the public school system is, after all, a reflection of ourselves a decade or so into the future; their reality is ours to be. The decade of blaming failures of public education on poorly-trained teachers, too much process and not enough substance, is the forerunner of the mounting attacks on the currently tenured faculty who are increasingly unable to effectively reach their students in this decade. The establishment-based beliefs of product and person need to be replaced by more institutional-based ones of process and situational ways of thinking.

Age/Gender/Culture Boundaries

The 1960s were about generational politics (Botstein, 1990). Although women and Blacks articulated the concepts, the youth, their attention galvanized by the Vietnam War, provided the idealism, energy and muscle to challenge the establishment defined by age: "You can't trust anyone over 30." The outlook was external; the university was largely united against those outside who exercised political and economic power and who were to be challenged. Of course, "they" were also on the Board of Directors and the university was the recipient of their "evil" money in the form of contract research, often from the Department of Defense. As a result, there were internal ramifications of these struggles. The focus of the anger, however, was outside; students and the new generation of young faculty were united. That scene was the end of the Modern Era; it was the final effort to claim an old dream. This form of generational politics is over; it has largely disappeared from the campus.

The 1990s are not an unfinished revolution as some would have us believe (Giddings, 1990; Bernstein, 1990; & DeMott, 1990). Such a view promotes self-deception among those who are now in positions of leadership that the experiences of their youth, and the world view they have carried into adult life, have continuity with the present and future. As a result they continue to try to persuade others to do specific things, such as adjust the curriculum, because it is "right," rather than because it is necessary. That is a mistake. Now is the start of something new; post-modernism is not about the discovery of correctness, it is about the adventure of moving from certainty into the unknown.

Thus, the conflict which in the '60s was externally directed, has now become internal. The geography of the struggle has moved to the campus and an emerging new clientèle of students has been joined by external forces to seek a reform of the internal system. The resistance from within is largely from older men who are in charge; but it is not their age and gender per se, i.e., men over 50, that are the central themes. People of all ages, races and gender face non-participation, enforced by change and by a world economy. The driving force for change is participation which is not linked exclusively to age or gender. The terms and conditions of the discourse have changed from moral to economic ends that the curriculum is to serve (Renner, 1993).

Summary

Curriculum issues are different than they have ever been before, certainly different than in the 1960s when it was proper to talk in terms of education (a philosophy of life), a product (what we need to know) and morality (what was right). This is no longer so. For the New Era we must dissolve the boundaries between: pure and applied (i.e., we need training to achieve education, not education as training); process and product (i.e., we need the process of how to know, not the discipline-based product of what we know); and age, gender and culture (i.e., we need a currency of interpersonal exchange based on fairly shared economic power and wealth, not moral philosophy). When we are able to adopt new beliefs, the content of the curriculum will have taken care of itself.

Diversity

In the 1960s gender and race was a moral issue. The ideal was a positive cultural value welded from individual spiritual commitments to "my brothers and my sisters all over this land," dissolving the fears and prejudice that for so long had separated us, as men/women and as majority/minority, one from another. But, it was not to be. Not enough individual acts of discovery were made to bring down the barriers of racism and sexism.

Even at places like Berkeley, which were successful in creating a numerical mix of race and gender, racial isolation is the legacy (Magner, 1990c). The pretext is over. Given the opportunity, people have made a choice for social distance while sharing physical proximity; neither whites or people of color, nor men or women, need be deceived any more about racism and sexism. Two black faculty members reflecting on their experiences over the past twenty years wrote: "For those of us who work in predominantly white institutions, feelings of isolation are our reality" (Dill & Dill, 1990). And, sexual assault continues to be a problem on campuses (e.g., Collison, 1991b; Sanday, 1990).

If we had done then, in the 1960s, what was right, making the moral commitment to social justice as a positive culture value, there now would be sufficient women and minority role models and 30 years later we would not be in the situation we are in, in which minorities (Bell, 1987) and women are still on the fringes (Blum, 1991; Leatherman, 1992). Over the period of affirmative action from 1970 to the present, the absolute number of white students enrolled in higher education has remained constant, while the absolute number of minority students has slowly increased, to now reach record numbers (Evangelauf, 1992a). The result has been a browning of the campus. These numbers, however, are misleading. Over this period of time, the number of whites in the general population has declined relative to the number of people of color. White enrollment has held its own through **increased** rates of participation, while minority participation rate has remained constant and enrollment has increased due entirely to greater absolute numbers, resulting from birth rate and immigration. Only whites in general and young white males in particular have made relative educational gains in higher education through more than two decades of affirmative action (Renner, 1993).

The response of minorities to being isolated and denied has been to move to a new level of consciousness that relinquishes acceptance (i.e., love) as the essential element, but which demands equal respect and participation. To such open expressions of reciprocal rejection, the reaction of the establishment is that the separatism of minorities and women from us is racist and sexist – i.e., that a Black Centre or a Women's Centre, and minority or women's studies programs, is as inappropriate as a white male student union or a white studies program and therefore should not be supported. The claim of a widespread backlash needs to be taken seriously (Faludi, 1991).

In the 1990s, gender and race have once again become a political issue. The real challenge of diversity is not simply counting among us increasing numbers of people of color, as well as women and the physically challenged, but of discovering conceptual ways of thinking and institutional practices which bind us to them economically and politically, not just socially (Renner, 1992). It is less important to eat and dance together (i.e., social integration as tolerance), than to work and live side-by-side with respect (i.e., economic integration of sharing wealth and political power as tolerance).

However, when diversity is taken out of this larger context, and is treated, as it is now, as a specialization, it becomes a head count: How many of each do you have, and what can we do to keep "them?" Unlike the 1960s, we will not have to do anything to achieve numerical diversity; from the 1990s on "they" will arrive. Higher education can use a 1960s mindset to stem the tide, as it is now doing by still seeing minority participation and retention as a student service and thus as a moral issue; but it shall be overcome. Now, the need is not to just figure out how to live with "them" (i.e., social tolerance), but also deal with "them" (i.e., share wealth and power in a meaningful way).

Diversity as "social tolerance" was as relatively painless as it was effective. But, as diversity is emerging as an issue of power and wealth in our nation and on our campuses there has been an eruption of racial incidents (Magner, 1989; 1990a; Shea, 1992) and a backlash against enforced "political correctness." White, straight, male and conservative forces have reacted to policies which protect minority rights as an infringement on freedom of speech and an intrusion on academic freedom (Wilson, 1989). The issue has moved from the pages of the *Chronicle of Higher Education* (e.g., Heller, 1990; Mooney, 1990) to a feature in *Time* (April 1, 1991) in the U.S., and in *Maclean's* (May 22, 1991) in Canada.

We should not be disturbed at one of the first signs that our universities may yet leave the sidelines to join in the battle of human existence marking the transition from one era to the next. We should only be discouraged that we are doing it so poorly; it would have been much easier to have completed then what was intended back in the 1960s.

Diversity in the curriculum is not about addition and subtraction. The issue is not what we should take out of the classic curriculum to replace with a better revisionist curriculum; both are equally and unavoidably ideological, as is life. But, as a zero-sum curriculum game, the arithmetic can only cause conflict over an issue without a correct answer. We have set ourselves up once again by defining the issue where the only choice is between unacceptable alternatives; the signposts for re-definition. If we can, instead, re-define the task as taking down the three barriers to knowledge posed by a curriculum driven by the ideologies of disciplines, students and faculty will be too busy learning in a variety of individually appropriate ways to quarrel over who is more right (Palmer, 1987). Who is "right" is a silly question for the New Era.

The re-definition, however, will not be possible as long as the academy is locked up tight, and those that were promised but denied participation from the 1960s on are on the outside looking in. Immediate financial and academic flexibility is required. We are experiencing the conflict between young/old, white/color and men/women that was so clearly warned against more than a decade ago by the Carnegie Council (1980).

Cost-Containment

The issue of the escalating salary cost associated with the age distribution of the faculty, and the resulting lack of academic flexibility, has already been discussed. This is a specific, local, internal issue over which there is a clear response. However, there are two additional aspects to cost-containment, both of which directly affect the substance of higher education.

Over-Management

In recessionary times the tendency is to hire more managers, and in particular administrative staff, to manage less, less well, further over-extending the institution. In the last 15 years investments in faculty salaries have increased by 21%; in administrative salaries, 42% (Halfond, 1991). The number of non-teaching staff (i.e., accountants, lawyers, system analysts) continues to grow faster than any other kind of employee according to a Federal study of 3300 colleges (Nicklin & Blumenstyk, 1993), including 4.5% for 91-92 despite the recession and mid-year reductions of appropriations by many states (Jaschik, 1992).

The principal danger is not so much the reduction in the absolute amount of money, but in what Halfond called the "insidious psychological aspects of bureaucracy." Over-management creates senseless systems which defeat the purposes for which they were intended. As the modern management literature has amply illustrated, over-management has contributed to the downfall of North American industry, and it is also doing so to higher education (see e.g., Lewis and Smith, 1994). As bureaucracy takes hold, organizational units become silos isolated from the common purpose of education, but similar in their effort to maintain themselves.

One illustration of what happens is when the notion of a "cost-centre" (an accounting concept) is carried beyond its logical limits, transforming organizational units from an educational to a bureaucratic focus. At one university where this happened, the Computer Centre started to give each faculty member one copy of the form required for processing exams to force a 10 cent photocopy charge (and to create a new task) back on to the department when a large volume printing would cost less than 2 cents each. Treating the teaching costs of each faculty member as a cost-centre makes little sense when most of the costs are for such items as handouts, examinations and grading which are dictated by class size set by the administration in the first place. The easiest way for a teacher to respond to pressure to reduce costs is to abuse the students sufficiently to reduce the class size or to neglect some aspect of teaching. The strategy of the library was to reduce hours at critical times. The crisis was then used to attempt to get a budget reinstatement by offering a choice between fewer hours or less journals (pitting student's interests against faculty interests). Seventy percent of the faculty now believe they work under autocratic management (Carnegie Foundation, 1989).

When bureaucracy takes hold, the substance of higher education suffers. In the examples given, limited fixed resources are charged back in an endless shuffle of paper money that create organizational silos isolated from shared educational purposes. Although Total Quality notions are now being discussed within academe, the applications have largely been applied to the operations side of the university; the substance of higher education – a student-focused attention to teaching and learning – is reduced by bureaucratic over-management.

Disestablishment

Thomas Langfitt (1991), a leader in the effort to control the escalating costs of higher education, has drawn a compelling comparison with the health care industry. In health care the costs have grown because health service institutions have competed with each other, not by containing costs, but by providing new facilities and adding expensive new diagnostic and treatment technologies. The more they compete the higher the costs. This has happened, in part, because we all want the best treatment, and physicians are seen publicly in the highly visible role of providing health; in contrast, what is done to promote the health industry is largely invisible, such as the duplication and over-use of expensive diagnostic services and increasing specialization in the practice and the science of medicine as opposed to direct service.

In short, the health industry is an "establishment" that has a life of its own. Large amounts of money are spent for "health" items that doctors, hospitals and researchers like to have, all very expensive, but which benefit relatively few. Whereas, most improvements in the physical health of a society are inexpensive changes in diet, sanitation and situational factors that are direct and easy to control (Miller, 1983). *Iatrogenesis* is the term for a health process that has the indirect result of causing or contributing to sickness (Illich, 1976).

The result has been a loss of confidence; 85% of Americans now believe there is a need for fundamental reform of the health care system. When those who have the power to make decisions about how this money is spent are seen as in a position of conflict of interests between what serves the health of people and what serves their own establishment, government intervention, regulation and loss of public confidence usually follows.

What is happening in higher education is similar (Langfitt, 1991). Costs of higher education escalated as colleges and universities competed with each other for the "best" faculty and students (Werth, 1988). A higher education "establishment" is one in which those who make decisions on how educational dollars shall be spent are the ones who will benefit most from decisions which maintain the establishment. Over the last decade the tuition and fees for higher education have increased faster than the rate of increases in cost for health care; and both exceeded the national rate of inflation. Nine out of ten Americans now think most people cannot afford to go to college without financial aid and six in ten believe that students have to rely too much on loans according to a 1990

Gallop poll (Manger, 1990b). If this continues, the net effect will be growing public impatience and eventual increased regulation similar to health.

Higher education is engaged in the "iatrogenic" process of using the power of the establishment to promote ignorance by needlessly restricting and locking-up knowledge and its use. As examples, this happens in the relative allocation to research as it competes with teaching functions. Another is the temporal delay required to first get a liberal education to qualify for a professional education which is a prerequisite for specialization permitting an apprenticeship which is a requirement for the certification allowing the actual use of the knowledge. Such credentialization also screens in favor of those with socio-economic positions of privilege and personal characteristics of compliance.

The issue is one of disestablishment. As long as those who will directly benefit from decisions have authority, and those who are affected by the decisions have either willingly relinquished involvement or are passively obedient, the outcome will be iatrogenic (Morgan, 1983). Disestablishment is a shift of power and wealth and is thus revolutionary in nature; the academic revolution is about a new paradigm, involving both new concepts of what is legitimate scholarship and knowledge, and new brokers (Boyer, 1990).

Summary

The substance of higher education is being diluted in largely invisible ways by the over-management of bureaucracy and by the self-interests of the establishment, at the loss of their opposites of community and institutional commitment to student-focused education. Both health care and higher education must either change from within or be changed.

Community

The starting point for a discussion of community is the Carnegie Foundation's (1990) report on *Campus Life: In Search of Community*. The six descriptive phrases they provided are absolutely and unequivocally essential; specifically, that a university or college:

- is an educationally purposeful community, a place where faculty and students share academic goals and work together to strengthen teaching and learning on the campus.

- is an open community, a place where freedom of expression is uncompromisingly protected and where civility is powerfully affirmed.

- is a just community, a place where the sacredness of each person is honored and where diversity is aggressively pursued.

- is a disciplined community, a place where individuals accept their obligations to the group and where well-defined governance procedures guide behavior for the common good.

- is a caring community, a place where the well-being of each member is sensitively supported and where service to others is encouraged.
- is a celebrative community, one in which the heritage of the institution is remembered and where rituals affirming both tradition and change are widely shared.

What a wonderful place to be; except it is gone from most of our four-year colleges and universities. There, the reality is one of growing intolerance (Magner, 1989) and what Boyer (1987) called "a house divided." Students are dissatisfied with large classes and the impersonal atmosphere of large universities (Wilson, 1991). Students' cynicism over being used is apparently well placed, because there is no evidence that the large, high-prestige research universities confer any advantage to their students in contrast to the lower-prestige teaching colleges which provide a more accessible and personal education experience (Pascarell & Terenzini, 1991). Faculty believe (Carnegie Foundation, 1989), and independent research confirms, that there is wide spread cheating in response to what students see as an uncaring and exploitive educational environment (Moffatt, 1990).

The exception to this loss of community is at two-year institutions where the Carnegie Foundation (1990) survey of campus life was struck by the frequency with which students spoke of experiencing community, of a place where faculty were "truly caring," and where they received in return the gratitude of *their* students. Thus, the ideal is not at issue, only a different understanding of how it is achieved. Community colleges seem to understand how to create the dynamics of a campus community.

As Naisbitt and Aburdene (1990) so clearly capture in *Megatrends 2000,* community is the voluntary association of individuals. In community there is no place to hide because everyone knows everyone else's business. People are linked and are inter-dependent. In such a system people feel and assume responsibility to and for each other. In contrast, in an impersonal environment, people can hide and avoid responsibility to and for each other. Those are the simple dynamics of community.

The espousal of the values alone may raise consciousness but will not accomplish very much; there must be opportunities for voluntary associations and the responsibilities they carry with them to capture the emerging personal motivations of the New Era. Because faculty and students have structured and formal connections through the curriculum and the classroom, this must become the mechanism for that end. To the extent that the goal is community, the curriculum must become a process not a product. In a very real sense, as Richard Elmore (1989) has written, "how we teach is what we teach."

For example, faculty report that the relative importance of the number of publications and of observations of teaching effectiveness for gaining tenure at two-year and four-year institutions is exactly the opposite, as shown in Figure 11-1. Faculty can not derive their identity from sources outside the university in the form of publications, as happens at four-year institutions, and yet expect

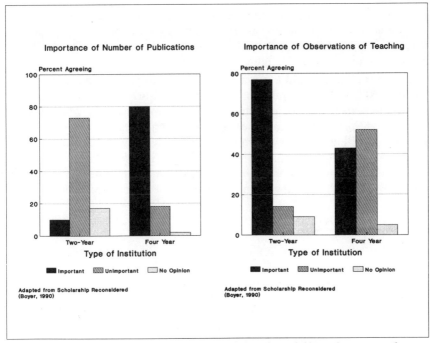

Figure 11-1: The Importance of Publications and Teaching

gratitude from a faceless and nameless class chasing a paper credential. If our students are to care about learning, we have to become inter-dependent enough to become a "purposeful community" by sharing academic goals and working with each other, as happens more often at two-year institutions. We must give our students the "justice" of a little respect for knowing what they want and what they need; they want the skills to participate.

The Blooms and Hirschs notwithstanding, the faculty cannot define the curriculum without regard to the players, any more than Masters and Johnson in their sex therapy program could treat one person for sexual dysfunction rather than a couple, because sex, like education, is an interaction. There is no such thing as an uninvolved teacher/learner.

For the New Era, the curriculum is to be founded in the laboratories of life; learning labs are not just for biology and chemistry. Collaborative learning (Whipple, 1987) is an adventure that starts with the decision by teacher and student to share an academic goal. When truly voluntary, it must match the needs of both the student and the teacher. This mutuality is far different than when "academic freedom" means my right as a teacher to do what I want and your right as a student to forego the credential that only compliance will bring.

Not long ago, the conceptual insight that a person should not have to kill themselves working in order not to starve to death brought about child labor laws and occupational health and safety. They were acts which we now call humanistic accomplishment, arising from a "simple" re-definition. The modern version is the inter-dependencies and collaboration out of which community comes – a person ought not have to return to the past in order not to be condemned to the past. The future is, after all, now.

If higher education did a better job of giving away knowledge instead of credentials, it may yet acquire the learners it so dearly desires. But, first the learners have to be free not to be the students we would have them be. Why are we so afraid of a purposeful, open, just, disciplined, caring and celebrative association with those who we would teach? Truly, how we teach is what we teach, and we are reaping what we have sowed; the first move is up to the faculty (us) toward community. It is very simple; if we choose to restore community, it is available; and, we will gain in the process a new measure of self.

Conclusions

The current agenda for higher education is for developing a coherent curriculum, accomplishing diversity, creating community and an achieving acceptable cost-containment to make it all possible. But like "love sweet love" knowing what we need and want is not enough. Although the list makes it relatively clear about what we need to accomplish, how to get there (the future) from here (now) is a problem. Just as there is a struggle over the details of the content, so too there will be an even bigger struggle over the process. The tough issues are not the technical ones about higher education; rather, they are the social and psychological ones about resisting primary change.

Chapter 12
The People
Social And Psychological Issues

The most striking feature about the crisis in higher education is its similarity with other social issues. Social issues are seldom complicated or hard to understand, nor are they beyond the reach of simple and feasible interventions (Seidman & Rappaport, 1986). Rather, their difficult nature comes from people and institutions being what they are. Both are remarkably resistant to changes which fundamentally alter the status quo.

Simply put, the problems of higher education are not technically complex or difficult, but they are profoundly social and psychological. The implications of this simple assertion are far reaching, requiring a framework that incorporates both psychology and political reality. It crosses the line between old science and New Era knowledge.

The forerunner of the current call (e.g., Cross, 1991; Grassmuck, 1990a) for a "new paradigm," had its beginnings in the late 1960s and early 1970s, when serious efforts were made to reconcile the irrelevance of social science research with the reality of the human social condition: racism, war, environmental deterioration and poverty to restrict the list to national concerns and to ignore the world problems of population, arms and hunger.

This effort was formalized in an emerging field called community psychology. Its concepts, values and strategies have provided an interface between psychology and power. When applied to higher education the effect is similar to the treatment of other recognized social issues: There is a clear problem which resists simple and feasible solutions primarily because of the nature of institutions and the beliefs and values of people – i.e., the possible solutions are not acceptable to those who have the capacity to bring them about. The solution, therefore, is a social, not a technical, issue.

Community Psychology

A community is any voluntary association of two or more people on any issue of mutual concern which makes them interdependent. Thus, it can include a marriage or a national revolution. It is not to be defined by geographic boundaries.

The independent decision for two or more people to voluntarily associate for some purpose reveals something about their motivation, and is thus psychological. These are whole people, not the divided-up parts of a person that make up the sub-disciplines of psychology, such as learning, perception, sensation, memory and cognition. To deal with people in life, however, we must put the parts together into a whole person, and then put the whole person into a social context with all of its complexity of politics, power and values. There are some guiding principles for combining psychology and life; there is, indeed, a handbook for the new academic revolution from within.

There are many similarities between the philosophy of knowledge explicit in community psychology with the messages coming from the Total Quality movement. Indeed, it is reasonable for the reader to treat this section as the psychology behind successful illustrations of the quality movement. In particular, it provides an explicit explanation of the psychological foundations of Deming's principles of "management by facts," "empowerment" and "freedom from fear" (Deming, 1986; see also Walton, 1986).

Primary Concepts

Our Relationships

Them/**Us**
Passive/**Active**

Our Problems

Technical/**Social**
Product/**Process**
Symptoms/**Causes**

Personal Change

Coercive/**Constructive**
Feasible/**Acceptable**

The Industry of Ideas

Bureaucratic/**Community**
Person/**Situation**
Manager of Change/**Agent of Change**

Process

Systemic/**Institutional**
Discovery/**Adventure**

Additional Concepts

Successive/**Simultaneous**
Competition/**Cooperation**

Box 12-1: Belief Templates

Show And Tell

The phrase "show and tell" was used by Julian Rappaport (1977) in the first comprehensive conceptual definition of the principles and assumptions of community psychology. This familiar phrase from pre-school education captures the essence of New Era science and knowledge. It is, in fact, a philosophy of science, a new paradigm in Kuhn's (1970) sense.

We are part of higher education. To act as if the issues of higher education can be defined as an objective, absolute topic, is to ignore that it is our beliefs, indeed our lives, that both direct, and are the objects of, our own study, confounding knowing with being. Because reflective analysis is not acceptable as science, we keep returning to "product" types of information, pretending that facts exist and we do not.

Community psychology has introduced the term action-research to help deal with the contradiction that, in the psychology of life (political reality), analysis and action are not separate in the ways the words "pure" and "applied" research would have us believe. Action-research treats knowledge as a process. For example, for Career Alternatives the primary research question is: Who at this particular university would be interested, under what conditions and what could be done about it here? The questionnaire to provide the answer is part of the intervention of raising the issue and informing individuals; thus, it is a means of manipulating the variable it is also designed to measure.

Action-research is empowering by drawing the participants together, as both the experimenter and the subject, into an analysis-information-action cycle. The crisis in higher education is a social and political process, as well as a substantive topic, and our tools and strategies must reflect this.

When giving a demonstration of Position Description Analysis, one administrator's comment was that he would like to have a spread sheet like that for *his* faculty in *his* top drawer, implying that it was for his eyes and his eyes only. However, to see the technique as a management tool, for masterfully confiscating redundant positions and distributing developmental ones with judicial insight, and for cleverly negotiating positions descriptions before advertisements were placed is to totally miss the point. That is the very old style of a manager of change which will not work; the challenge of leadership is to become an agent of change.

The place for the Position Description Analysis spread sheet is painted on the side of the administration building for all to see. The state of the professorate at that institution then becomes everyone's business and responsibility, including recognizing the potentials for cooperation and the constraints on change. Everyone would know how many claim to be good at what, and some might even find, much to their surprise, that there are others with whom they might like to talk, to list two possibilities.

However, it is hard to be both the researcher (or manager) and the researched (or managed); our philosophies of science and management keep trying to separate the two. The point can be illustrated clearly in the work that I did with a police department on their relations with the minority community on the issue of excessive use of force.

On two occasions, after questionable incidents involving the use of force in the Black community, the police had been fired upon when responding to a call. A Black leader said to me, as a university professor who does action-research, we have to do something or someone is going to get killed. I thought about the problem. I said, if assaulting a police officer or resisting arrest is a characteristic of the citizen, rather than the policeman, then each officer who is doing equivalent patrol should have an equal chance of being sent to the scene.

The police department initially had no interest in cooperating with this research study; but, the court docket was public information. We looked at every entry on the docket over a several year period and recorded the name of the officer for every charge of resisting arrest or assaulting a police officer. We used political means to get access to assignments to patrol duty. We calculated the necessary probability distributions. One officer on the force had one chance in one million of coming across so many difficult people; two others, one chance in 10 000 (Renner & Gierach, 1975). The best guess was that the difficulty was with the officers not the citizens. Some combination of the three policemen were involved in both of the questionable incidents which had led to a subsequent ambush.

We then took our results to the police command. One officer said: "If we are honest with ourselves we know those three are our problem men and we have not done anything about it; I think we should cooperate. What additional records do you need?" My response was: "None. If we do these kinds of studies we will only ruin your records because your officers will change the paper trace. There is nothing you can do with the information. You have no direct control over what they do because their work is largely invisible (similar to academic work), except for the paper." For example, an officer I later heard say "it is the 27th I better give out tickets or I'm not going to make quota" stood out in a probability distribution based on frequency of tickets by day of the month.

The command asked what I would suggest. I proposed that any future probability studies should only be done by a code number known only to each officer and not to the command. The command agreed, and I was given access to each patrol shift to show and tell the results and to explain the rules for any future work. In the presentation I pointed out that any one in the room could have been the one to be shot at; they carry each other's grief. Once the problem was re-defined this way, and once they all knew about their collective behavior and each one of them about their own behavior, it was *their* responsibility, not the command's. This was a community of inter-dependent individuals looking to each other to solve their problems. The policeman who gave out tickets in mass after the 27th of each month had to decide whether he was going to continue to be that kind of person; the answer was no. The officers themselves formed a community relations program to work out their differences with the minority community; on this project no order for change was ever issued by the command.

We later described this as doing research "with" not "on" people, as a kind of knowledge that is respectful of others (Sherwin & Renner, 1979). In their book on community psychology, O'Neill and Trickett (1982) have compiled examples like this one to illustrate the principles for creating a sense of community within a setting. The choices we made followed from an appreciation that social problems are both psychology and politics; they are about actual people in specific settings. So too, with Position Description Analysis. Although it is a tool concerned with issues of higher education, the issues exist at institutions. Social problems are not faceless; they reflect the way individuals act in their everyday life. There can only be participants; those who are to be the results must also be the researchers.

Evaluation

Another variation on this process is a form of evaluation research espoused by Pat Cross (1987; 1988; 1990). We already know enough about learning styles and teaching methods for each faculty member to put in place an evaluation process which would turn each of our individual classrooms into a learning laboratory, uniting instructor and students as cooperative partners. Only students in our own classes can tell *us* how to best teach *them*, thus allowing for the wide range of individual differences known to exist among them as students and us as teachers (Kolodny, 1991). The process is to ask at the end of each class three questions to which each student writes down and hands in their answer: (1) What was the lesson of today's class? (2) What didn't I understand? (3) What do I want or need to know more about?

This knowledge is a classroom-based process, and at the same time an intervention that eliminates blaming and does not treat achievement as a scarce resource to be won by a few in competition with others. Instead we obsess over meaningless measurements, such as making better exit exams to label a few as exceptional on a criterion that is artificial, all in the name of standards. A little good evaluation type of action-research could allow us to actually achieve the standards.

The challenges facing higher education are relatively few and quite specific, such as more effective teaching and meaningful learning. If we will treat data which is designed to inform decisions as "real" knowledge, and suspend our unbending commitment to hypothesis testing and theory driven "product" types of knowledge, we can then deal directly with a wide variety of social issues. What I have described are processes based on knowledge as an adventure arising from assuming the role of an agent of change.

Involvement

One of the powers of action research and evaluation as a show and tell process is involvement. For example, one of the results of the process of Position Description Analysis is that every person either gives themselves a "name" (or someone will call them one) of up to three, eight digit numbers. In one procedural step there is no such thing as an uninvolved participant.

Just as all the policemen looked for the position of their own code number on a probability distribution, because it is human nature, so too will all the faculty have some stake in identifying the current roles and functions and debating the ideal. The knowledge (i.e., the research product) and the process are not separable. Of course the rules are very important. For each policeman it was important that neither the command nor others knew their individual code number. Each person had to be safe from being singled out; in that safety was the freedom to choose to change as a self-determining act. Likewise, if Position Description Analysis (like my administrator wanted) is a hit list, it will cause more trouble than it does good, and it will be impossible to know what it is that needs to be known because individuals will hide the information; product and process interact as they always will.

A simple evaluation strategy at the end of each class makes each student responsible, too, not just the professor. It is the beginning of a dialog; there is no such thing as an uninvolved partner in a learning experience. For this to happen the professor does not need to know the name of the student, and in a similar way, neither the Dean nor the Chief of Police should even want to know the name of any individual on the list; there is little useful they can do with the information, but much harm. General descriptive knowledge – as public information which takes show and tell to the limit – is essential. If every student and the professor in a given class knew that 90% of the students said "you mumble too much and I can't read your hand writing," then it would hard for both to continue to meet in the same classroom in unacknowledged silence, without coming to terms with the information.

Responsibility

People often hate responsibility when they have it – it makes them work hard, be involved and care; but they are deeply unhappy, frustrated and alienated when they do not have it. Such is the love/hate affair with responsibility. Large and impersonal institutional settings with specialized roles and functions allow people to escape responsibility.

The opposite is true for a community. What we do is visible to others and what they do to us. Because there is no escape we form relationships with others to acknowledge our inter-dependency and the responsibilities and mutual benefits it brings. Show and tell is a process which enhances visibility.

To associate with another in some activity or enterprise is to choose not to be invisible. The choice itself, a self-determined act, is to gain a sense of self, for it is now clear both to the individual and to others who the real person is. We make character attributions about others when their actions are seen to be an expression of themselves, independent of the situation; when the situation makes a strong demand (i.e., they had no choice, everyone would do that), then we do not feel we know much about that individual's personality.

Increased involvement and greater responsibility are the instrumental effects of "show and tell," achieved through action-research and local evaluation. Although data-based activities, these are also the psychological ways in which a setting creates "community." Old science treats such data as low level applied research, but for the social and political reality of a New Era, such efforts are the means of choice to create useful new knowledge. There can no longer be a distinction between learning and living, and we can best teach that lesson by living it ourselves. It requires only simple existing tools; it does not require new resources, just the understanding that the dynamics of human life in social settings and political reality can not be separated without doing violence to the unity that is both mover and object (Sarason, 1972; 1978).

Relationships

The academic version of the old philosophical question: "If a tree falls in the woods and no one is there to hear it, does it make a noise?", is if a professor gives a lecture and no one comes, listens or learns, did he teach?

Involvement and responsibility require both "us" and others; they are about relationships, and in particular voluntary ones. We need others to define ourselves, as is captured in the refrain from the song by America: "In the desert you can't remember your name, cause there ain't no one to give you no pain." The joys of teaching are the effect on students, and through this relationship the emancipation of cognitive and spiritual resources. The student's learning does not diminish the teacher – teaching and learning is not like conservation of energy – but rather it is the relationship that enables both. It is a dynamic process (Shulman, 1987; 1989).

To the extent that contemporary colleges and universities have allowed us to avoid relationships with our students and each other, we have been protected from involvement and responsibility. For example, administrators and faculty do not see or feel the frustration at registration caused by course decisions made for budget reasons at a distant times and places, any more than "carpet" or "surgical" bombing is a personal act. Conversely, involvement and responsibility breeds the necessity for relationships.

Inter-dependency

The mechanism for a cooperative relationship is inter-dependency; if two people will link their fate, each acquires capacity from the other. Two people of different races will become the best of buddies by putting them together in a trench during war where the survival of the one is essential to the survival of the other. The principal extends to institutions as well; the Persian Gulf war produced some remarkable pairs of national buddies. The same principles are much easier to apply in the less extreme circumstances of gaining cooperation for responding to the issues of higher education. In fact, wise people will often choose to create such inter-dependent arrangements.

Career Alternatives are simply one of the means for both those who are "tired" and those who are still "keeners" to share a single common purpose of a new lease on life. Instead, we struggle over whether those who are not active "enough" in research should teach an additional course (a punishment) or whether someone else's program should be reduced so ours can grow. Such contingency structures are prescriptions for conflict by blocking inter-dependency and fostering competition where cooperation is required.

Persons and Situations

As people, we give too much credit to the personal characteristics of others and not nearly enough to the situation. Social psychologists call this the fundamental attribution error. For ourselves, each of us feels all of the external pressures to do this or that. But, for others, all we see is their actions. For example, more students want a practical education. And, we make attributions about them, such as students these days have the wrong motivations for higher education, to paraphrase the results of the Carnegie survey of faculty attitudes.

Problems arise when individuals make decisions based on those attributions, such as concluding that students really need a good liberal education, and then give them more of what they are reacting against, which to their surprise, does not solve the problem. For example, students have started to cheat more

(Carnegie Foundation, 1989; Collison, 1990; Moffatt, 1990). The solution colleges and universities have discovered is to push the source of the problem deeper into the educational system and insist on better teacher training so the students will come better prepared for what we are prepared to teach. Thus, higher education is absolved of any further responsibility, except to be patient and understanding while waiting for a better supplier.

This is an example of coercive rather than constructive problem solving. The starting place for re-definitions are the beliefs and attributions which ignore the situation. If what we teach has little direct bearing on life and introduces needless temporal delays between learning and doing, then, of course, our efforts will be resisted. We already know that students will flock to classes that are connected to life, even if they involve considerable work and risk – such as giving a public comedy routine at a pub. They are classes, however, that few are prepared to teach. But, humor is like a tree falling in a distant forest if it can not be put to use in the context of therapy or marketing as well as entertainment. The students will come back to the basics of an old style liberal education when they need them, and not before.

People have good survival instincts; they do not pass up a chance to get what they need and want. It is often a lot easier to change the situation to fit the person, then to either change the person or to make them do what they do not want to do.

Security

People do not take significant personal risks without security; to free a person to change, it is necessary to make the situation safe to try an alternative. In his discussion of a Career Alternatives program, O'Neill (1988) called this "unfreezing" the environment. A Career Alternative has the effect of giving flexibility to the institution and to the person. It links the mutual benefits of both into one action, giving both the necessary security to take a risk. At present there is a bad fit between some people and the institution. No one needs to be blamed for this; it is a simple show and tell fact with a quite reasonable historical explanation. All that is required is to link their fates so that both are free to make new choices. It is good social psychology to fix conditions so that the people who share a setting have the security to make choices that are in each others' mutual interest.

Utility Theory

Our actions always carry with them contingent outcomes. This is not something that is either good or bad, it is a fact of life. The only questions to be asked are: What are the current situational contingencies and what actions do they support or suppress?

Self-regulation is when we make deliberate use of these facts on ourselves. When I could not seem to remember my own office number, I asked the secretary not to do anything for me if I could not tell her first my office number.

It took me one trip back to my office to read the number on my own door to learn 3417 to my dying day.

When four of us team-taught a personality course we added an item to the standard student course evaluation form asking the students to rank order the four of us. Each term one of us would be first and someone last, and there was no way any of us intended to be last on any list. It was not by accident that the course became the most popular one in the department – it was extremely well taught. Life is full of consequences. Tell me your expressed ideals, show me your contingencies, and I will tell you whether you "kid me not."

Two Variations: Competition and Cooperation

Once we say "this university cannot be all things to all people," then none of us can admit to be less than perfect, and we will compete against each other till death do us part. In *practical* terms, competition has not always been bad; it has created our modern university: Higher education in the U.S. and Canada is respected world-wide, there is an unequalled research establishment, demand is growing and most agree our higher education system is essential for the nation to remain competitive in a world economy. That is a very good position. However, resources are now shrinking and competition is destructive of community under these new conditions.

We need to believe that the status quo is over. We can choose to go down with the ship, fighting for our space in the life boat; that is the competitive choice. The alternative is to re-define the situation. We can even agree with those in the life boats that the university cannot be all things to all people, that we are in a negative growth situation for the next decade at a minimum and that we did this together. The re-definition, however, is that we are all in this to the end together. Some departments are up, some are down, but the best individual hope is for the whole to be healthy. With this belief there is security and with it room to bring down some of the artificial lines between disciplines. For example, there can be room for theatre in business, and as a result the Senate will not have to debate closing the Art Centre because it cannot make it as a user-pay cost-centre; or, for part of medicine or business to be in philosophy because ethical analysis in all spheres is becoming a growth industry, to mention a few of the obvious.

This alternative model is cooperative. A humor course cross-listed as business and clinical psychology is proper, even if it uses a half line now empty in both departments to keep theatre in operation. Dynamism feeds itself. To break the retrenchment cycle offers both business and psychology the potential to recover the half line, and we are all richer for the viable Art Centre as a resource for campus life.

There is not much of a choice for higher education: Either change or be changed. The bottom line is, which one? If we will choose to change from within, then we must do it in a way that preserves the academic values we share. The model is cooperative, and the question is how to arrange the internal situation to gain financial, academic and management flexibility to invest in dynamism.

The steps are straightforward. If Career Alternatives are a possibility, then the question becomes: What needs to be in place at this university for that to work? If cooperation is a goal, what do we need to do to create academic budgets that support academic roles and functions? What are the conditions under which it is safe for a department to admit to being less than perfect through Position Description Analysis as the best way to allow visions and pockets of dynamism to develop? The old way of punishing honesty through cannibalization of the position will not work. The academic budgets implied in Position Description Analysis have the capacity to give expression to the pursuit of academic values.

Two Questions

There is no single correct incentive structure. For any individual to believe they know which one is correct is to start a debate that has no end. The task of creating and evaluating workable incentive structures, however, unlike most policy discussions in the faculty senate, can be debated and acted upon. There are two questions to ask:

- What are the consequences of our current polices and structures, i.e., what actions do they support or suppress?

- What consequences would produce or suppress any given desirable outcome? (*Not* a debate over which one of two desirable outcomes is more important – e.g., books or computers.)

These are not difficult questions to answer. A descriptive look at the way past budget wars have been fought will go a long way toward answering the first question. The answer to the second question can be evaluated against the fairly objective standards of fairness and whether the procedures can be exploited. Good teachers, parents and leaders make these analyses all the time. Their efforts fail when power is used authoritatively to manage (control) others, as in managing change. Their efforts are most effective when they are a form of self-regulation, fairly and evenly administered by an agent of change – one who relinquishes authority over the outcome in order to gain control through expanding what others have accepted responsibility for.

Sabotage

Part of a good incentive system is to cut off trouble at the pass. Once the basic structure is in place, the next question is to ask how someone can do it in. If there are 50 ways to leave your lover, there are a least a ten ways to sabotage these approaches as applied to the three challenges. The first antidote is to clearly label them, thus making it harder for someone to use the trick without detection, and the second is to build into the system contingencies that make sabotage counter productive or risky.

Steal the Savings

What happens if government wants to keep the money? The simple answer is there must be a line item in the operations budget called "the future fund" where flexibility dollars go and come from. In public universities this requires a public political deal. All the players have a vested interest in getting higher education unstuck, and all have a stake in making the savings do the job they were intended to do. Hard, clear, open, public bargaining is required; no one, but no one, should be able to get paranoid about the process. If they can, the bargaining is not finished.

Know What is Best

Someone, to be sure, will know what is correct; but that is old science. For this reason, adopting the belief that this is the end of the Modern Era is critical. In a New Era, there is no truth, only adventures. By the definition of Post-Modern, the correct answer cannot be known in advance, therefore there is only process. The vocabulary is restricted to: this is interesting, this is integrative, this is exciting, this is outrageous; but *never*, this is correct.

Hedge on Security

Academic colleagues often tell me the university can't promise that no one will be fired as a result of the process, often followed by "because we have to set some priorities." Few business people have any trouble understanding the need for security. Deming made it a fundamental requirement for achieving quality (Walton, 1986). Vertical cuts in academia will be cost-ineffective because they do not solve the underlying structural problem. There is a fixed price to be paid for the recovery of the savings; this is an investment price that is part of any venture deal. If an institution can't risk the price it can't play the game, because hedging on security makes the effort to change a bad risk, and therefore one which should not be taken. It is not in anyone's interest for a hedge on security.

Manipulate Information

Life in a community is life in a fishbowl; they go together. The right to know takes precedent over individual privacy, which is one reason why individual security must be ironclad tight. We have made progress in affirmative action by the concept of systemic discrimination based solely on outcome, which requires public and open accountability. Show and tell goes to the limit. Competing data bases are a frequent and desirable outcome. If the student union published course evaluations by faculty names that is fine; if a department wants its own evaluation questions, that is fine. But, neither is the official, legitimate or correct one; they are just different ones. The information age is about information, open and on deck, no fiddling.

Covet and Compete

"We need to set priorities" is a hard phrase to eliminate, but no one is allowed to use it in its usual context. In a cooperative, the savings accruing to a member belong to the member to be invested in ways that serve the member, and the savings cannot be taken by someone else because of the argument that their own ends are more important. On the other hand, how the cooperative will decide to advance its collective self with the communal share of the individual efforts will, of course, involve competition and politics, but not in ways that are destructive. Those that stand to gain the most from the successful individual efforts of the collective, can best advance their own cause by helping each individual member to thrive.

Confuse Process and Product

Old science ways of thinking want rational and deductive answers. However, fundamental change comes from creative and inductive leaps of faith. Definitive scholarship is not nearly as important as the exercise of collecting information to inform decisions. When the task is to cut with an axe there is no need to measure with an micrometer. The academic mind can hold up progress in the search for needless perfection without equal from any quarter.

Try to Change Someone Else First Rather Than Self

At a criminal justice conference I attended, correction personnel said prisons failed because judges sent too many people to jail causing overcrowding, judges said the police brought too many to court, police said the public demanded tough enforcement, and the public said mothers and families were no longer instilling social values in their children. As the commentator I added the final line: "Until mothers stop having babies there is no solution to correctional reform and overcrowding in prison." This is nonsense. Each level has its own roles and responsibilities, and that is where everyone starts. Otherwise responsibility is diluted and it is up to someone else, first. The academic version is that we could teach better if the students were better prepared in high school. And it is also true that our problems would be solved if mothers stopped having babies.

Wrap up in the Robes of Tenure and Academic Freedom

Just about everything is potentially covered by this one. It is time to remember that the purpose of tenure and academic freedom is to protect the expression of unpopular ideas and to engage in unorthodox scholarship. As O'Neill (1988) noted, it is the supreme irony that the tenure system, which is supposed to allow intellectual ferment, may have actually given us the environment of the good citizen. He asks: "Of what value is it to protect the rights of senior faculty to express radical opinions when they had to demonstrate that they did not have any radical opinions before they could get tenure?" It is time to go the wall for anyone who will challenge the status quo under the banner of academic freedom, and to start dealing separately with the issues of economic security for what they actually are – i.e., providing reasonable and practical conditions of employment security which are a perquisite for creating fundamental change.

Set Up Conflicting Camps by Creating Either/or Decisions

The classic one is to set up such things as pay raises and tuition increases as either/or choices and to divide students and faculty, or set the choice as diluting quality versus instituting more use-pay fees for incidentals. The rules have to preclude the capacity to stiff someone else by setting up such dilemmas. The dilemma those within higher education have given themselves is on a grand scale of the choice between either internally-directed retrenchment or government intervention. When such forced choices are offered, the response has to be to reject both alternatives and to seek re-definition within constraining principles, such as: Faculty deserve competitive fair wages. Students are not be gouged. Yearly tuition increases are to be linked to inflation, and absolute levels set to reflect the politics of access.

Conclusions

This book is a guide to thinking; it is not a handbook. The technical tools are useful as starting places, but not as something to be followed like a recipe. There are as many unique manifestations as there are applications. In fact, to follow the suggestions explicitly will assure that there would never be any exact replications, and therefore, under the rules of old science, no legitimate knowledge. Once the process is started the only ideas that have currency are local ones, i.e., the means, ends and processes that people are uniquely prepared to deal with.

Chapter 13
The Organization
Management Issues

In the 1980s U.S. industry began switching from vertical to horizontal organizational structure in response to the competition from Japan. The first response was to copy the techniques – e.g., quality circles – but such efforts often failed because they were imposed on the traditional vertically-organized bureaucratic structure that had served U.S. industry so well through the final phase of the Industrial Revolution. Now, successful industries in global competition have transformed their organizational structures as well.

Similar to all ideas, the organizational system based on a rational structure and a hierarchical line of authority has had its time and place. Bureaucracies reformed the previous corruptions of government and the inefficiencies of their industrial predecessors, and accommodated well the requirements of growth and the economy of size, perhaps illustrated best by General Motors. However, a bureaucracy works through the application of rules and it advances people who play by those rules. As the status quo becomes entrenched, the bureaucratic/professional way of thinking becomes a template through which creativity is stifled and the vitality of renewal is attenuated. In times of reform, efficiency is of greatest value; in times of revolutionary change, vitality and creativity are essential.

Although the management revolution has started to spread into the health and service sectors, it has been resisted in a fundamental way by government and by higher education, both of which continue to do business as usual. This is not to say that the "buzz-words" of the emerging post-bureaucracy era – such as empowerment, quality and accountability – have not been introduced into university life. They have been, but their implications for actual organizational change have not.

Managers in higher education need a perspective to guide their actions. The translation of the assumptions, beliefs and approaches of this monograph into a post-bureaucratic management philosophy can be illustrated through a discussion of Total Quality Management (TQM) and Feminism, both of which have claimed to offer insight into how higher education can join in the transition from vertical to horizontal. This is the kind of organizational change that marks the end of the Modern Era and, for want of a better term, the beginnings of the Post-Modern.

Total Quality Management

Total Quality Management (TQM) – in theory – should be good for higher education. In fact, colleges and universities which have introduced TQM processes have no difficulty in providing examples of applications to accounting, operations and physical plant areas where universities and business are similar. Often the financial savings have been substantial (Whittington, 1992).

The problem, however, is in figuring out how to apply the concepts to the academic "product" of higher education – teaching and learning (Carothers, 1992; Marchese, 1991, 1992). Good illustrations of academic applications are few and far between. In part, this is because professors are driven by promotion, tenure and discipline-based standards, and in part, because curriculum improvement is seldom either continuous or customer driven (Cornesky, McCool & Weber, 1992).

When pushed for academic illustrations, the examples that are given may seem trivial – such as conducting a survey to find that professors were frustrated because erasers were dirty and chalk was missing from the classroom (Whittington, 1992). The solution of caddies which hold a week-long supply of chalk, in the context of strong external demand for greater accountability, cost-containment, smaller class size, more learning and better service to more diverse students, seems to miss the essence of what quality improvement is about.

The specific problem with chalk exists on many campuses. It is, perhaps, a better example of costly and unproductive cycles that have been introduced into academic life through over-management and uncritical budget cuts, and of why there is a need for TQM. The missing chalk only became a problem in the first place when cleaning was reduced to a weekly affair, resulting in dirty, under-serviced classrooms.

Good TQM – management by facts – would have first asked: What will happen when classrooms are serviced less often? The predictable answer is the supply of chalk will become unpredictable. What is now

Primary Concepts
Our Circumstances
General/**Specific**
National/**Local**
External/**Internal**
Our Relationships
Them/**Us**
Passive/**Active**
Our Problems
Technical/**Social**
Product/**Process**
Symptoms/**Causes**
Organizational Change
Secondary/**Primary**
Successive/**Simultaneous**
The Industry of Ideas
Bureaucratic/**Community**
Person/**Situation**
Manager of Change/**Agent of Change**
Process
Systemic/**Institutional**
Discovery/**Adventure**

Box 13-1: Belief Templates

evident, after the fact, is that chalk caddies and an ethic of user-servicing (just like at McDonald's) are necessary components of reduced maintenance. Everyone who has been teaching throughout the period of retrenchment has stories of such cost-ineffective past decisions, some of which have been repaired, but most of which have not.

Certainly, we need to solve these past problems and stop creating new ones – and the TQM process can help – but on the fundamental issue of greater academic accountability, Total Quality Management is not about fixing what need not have been broken in the first place. And it is most certainly not about making it easier to continue to teach **with** chalk, when that is one of the problems with the current teaching and learning experience in the first place (while still allowing that chalk should be there). True TQM would take us from where we are (teaching with chalk) to where we need to go (better teaching and learning involving both the use of appropriate technology and substance which is inclusive of adult learners and the twenty-something generation).

Defining Academic Quality

Part of the difficulty arises from the ambiguous nature of the product of teaching and learning. It will be hard to improve "productivity" if there is very little agreement on what is to be improved and on what improvement is. For example, having standing-room only in a course increases the teacher/student ratio, but it is not an improvement in the true sense of quality even though the department has higher productivity and is now more cost-effective than last term. If the longer-term consequences are lower rates of retention in students, poor morale, a bad reputation and future alumni who don't give, the ratio was indeed far from a useful measure on which to have based departmental budgets which rewarded that "solution." Yet, such is the result when pressures for cost-effectiveness are passed down the hierarchy, much like quotas on the old productions lines. Clearly, definitions and standards are an important issue.

Fundamental to even thinking about applying TQM to academic issues is an unequivocal commitment to *identify and to respond to customer requirements.* That is the biggest stumbling block for academics. From the results of the Carnegie surveys we know that faculty believe students are poorly prepared, need a liberal education and are too career oriented. However, from Astin's annual surveys of college freshmen, we know that students regard themselves as well prepared, want a relevant education and see the purpose of college and university as preparing them for a career.

So far, these conflicting attitudes, and the definitions and standards they imply, have been played out within academia as philosophical debates about what is correct. As philosophical debates, there can not be any answer in the form of a "benchmark" standard. The correct answer in any rational analysis always depends on what were the underlying assumptions, which, because they are assumptions, can never be facts. However, management by facts – one of the principles of TQM – requires information not philosophy. Thus, academic applications of TQM principles will require the definition of significant academic issues in a such a way that one can measure how close existing practice comes to a desired standard. One such measurement tool is Position Description Analysis, and it provides one illustration of how a TQM process can be applied to academic issues.

Position Description Analysis (PDA)

Position Description Analysis was described in Chapter 9 as an approach for mobilizing change, i.e., it provides both facts and a process for change. It does not take very long for the power of PDA to be quite transparent. Someone's academic area of specialization (not a specific person) will be "surplus" – but of course, specific people will be in those specializations, and they may feel like they are on a redundancy list. The discrepancies on the spreadsheet will depend on who defines the "ideal," opening the possibility that others, beyond the faculty, now have a quite specific means to identify their needs. For example, the procedure can be used to describe the actual set of course descriptions which are offered and the ideal ones from the point of view of the student consumer. Obviously, discrepancies can be calculated between the different ideals of students and faculty as well as between each of those ideals and the actual. It is clear as well, that when needs are so explicitly defined they can be translated into hiring criterion for replacement faculty; as a result, the hiring process can be less political and more information based. These are but a few of the implications of the impact of PDA on people and their relationships with each other within an institution. PDA exemplifies the requirement for open and joint consideration of information and how it is to be used.

Total Quality as a Process

In addition to the definitions and standards, there is the second, equally important, consideration of recognizing that TQM is a process. This means simply that people have to participate and cooperate. And this, in turn, requires understanding people and their relationships to each other within a particular setting.

However, a "product" type of mind-set runs deep, along two parallel channels of thinking, one grounded in scholarship and one in application. Of course, both scholarly and applied perspectives are legitimate in their own right; but they are problematic if the goal is to use PDA as a process in a TQM context. Specifically:

When we were developing the procedure, colleagues would question whether the catalog was definitive, and whose definition of future academic needs would be most valid. These were requests for absolute judgements about the content from a perspective of *scholarship*. But, when the goal is to start a local process, it does not matter if the catalog is not the final word from a philosophy of knowledge standard. Epistemologists will be debating that problem long into the future. The only issue is whether PDA can be used reliably for the intended purposes of a personnel resource audit. The answer is clearly yes, in the sense that libraries and professional associations organize information so we can find a book or group of like-minded colleagues at a conference without major difficulty.

In contrast, from an *applied* perspective, administrators immediately see the power of the information for allocating limited resources and targeting retrenchment decisions. PDA provides the kind of information that an institution needs for rational decision making. However, these applications are from a management perspective and PDA should never be used as a "management" technique, because if it is, it is doomed to fail. Once it becomes the means for a "hit list" for next round of budget cuts, its usefulness will be undermined.

There are many ways PDA can be sabotaged; it will not survive a hostile environment. Thus, the value of PDA can never be solely in the information, but also from the act of participation in an analysis of needs and capacity, which is a process. The primary management objective must be in doing the exercise so that everyone has a clear descriptive picture and a shared responsibility and ownership of the implications. The main objective cannot be to use the information administratively, only to start the process.

Six Principles

There are six principles for the application of TQM to academic issues which can be illustrated through PDA:

1. **TQM has open-ended consequences**. This means the process has to be neutral at the start; it cannot be biased for any specific person to achieve their own specific ends. No actual power can be hidden or even implied for the personal gain of some at the peril of others. In Deming's terms, there must not be fear of the consequences. If there is, then participation in the process will be resisted.

In the case of PDA there must be absolute assurance that no faculty member will be dismissed (or involuntarily assigned new duties) through use of the information. No administrator may have any authority to directly use the information. The reasons are two-fold: without freedom from fear, the information that is needed will not become available; and the purpose is not to administratively use the information but to share ownership of a problem, which is necessary to effectively make use of the knowledge in any case.

2. **TQM is participatory**. This means that everyone who would be affected by the process has the means and the motivation to participate in those processes that affect them. Administrative pronouncements of a commitment to participatory management alone are not enough. Genuine participation leading to effective change is a movement, and a movement is based on wide-spread and meaningful involvement.

In the case of PDA there are no uninvolved "bystanders." Unlike Senate debates which selectively attract participants on the basis of self-interest, PDA applies to everyone at the same time, and everyone has a vested interest in exactly what 8-digit code numbers they are going to be assigned. The personal response is: "No one is going to catalog me as a 24-12-11-02, without my participation."

3. **TQM is dynamic.** This means that the exercise is clearly important and addresses the essential nature of an important problem with instrumental consequences. Something will happen at the end as a result of the exercise.

In the case of PDA the potential consequences are real and will affect the people who are objects of the exercise. No faculty member can afford to ignore how the emerging future of his or her discipline is defined. Future appointments and the curriculum, to mention only two, hang in balance.

4. **TQM is empowering.** This means that those who are most affected are the ones who have the capacity to turn the resulting information into instrumental acts. If ownership of a problem is to be assumed by the individuals responsible for the product, then they must have the power to use the information to effect change. Since the faculty control many academic decisions, ultimately they must be the ones to take ownership and to make the essential choices. The only other alternative is try to move the locus of power up the administrative hierarchy. When that has been tried it has been a source of administration/faculty conflict and has not worked. Shifting the power balance toward greater administrative authority is favored by many Board members, and increasingly by government, and may yet be elevated to a new round of confrontation if higher education can not find an internal way to achieve greater external accountability to the requirements of their variety of customers (in its broadest sense including students, parents, employers and government).

In the case of PDA, I have suggested that to be useful it must always be linked to the budgets of individual units in two ways. First, any savings resulting from the use of the information goes to the units responsible for achieving cooperation and avoiding duplication, and second, the new flexibility must be invested in moving toward their ideal. When the only way the information can be used is for each unit to become less like the past and more like the future, then there are positive incentives for each unit to know itself in a publicly demonstrative way. With PDA the greatest potential comes from exposing discrepancies between future needs and current capacity, whereas, under retrenchment, there is a need to hide such discrepancies.

5. **TQM is a process.** This means that management has to make a commitment to support ends that are unknowable at the outset. The old way is for management (often through participation) to define the ends which are the definitions and standards of productivity, and then to devise a strategy to get there, again often with participation. Although there is a place for strategic management, the newer way is to create a process that has the power to create specific changes the nature of which cannot be identified in advance. In times of reform, when only secondary change is needed to solve known problems, the former may work when management has power and compliance, but the

latter is necessary in revolutionary times when those factors are absent, as is now the case in academic life.

The aspect of PDA that can be generalized from one setting to another is how to create the spreadsheet underlying the human resources audit. It is not the specific answers that are important. It does not matter that two different institutions will revise the procedure and that their results will not be directly comparable. A comparative national descriptive inventory of academic resources is a theoretical exercise of limited practical value. No one has any power to make any useful decision on such national norms using PDA. The only real value is at each local application. It is the process of a campus passionately examining its needs and capacities that creates the possibility of dynamic change within the existing structure of how academic decisions are actually made at individual institutions of higher education.

6. **TQM changes the institutional culture**. This means that destructive internal competition and lack of cooperation become less functional. Units of the organization begin to look at their inter-dependencies and work together toward better achievement of all of the components that add up to quality and reduced waste.

In the case of PDA, the phrase: "we need to set some priorities," in its traditional meaning, will be dropped from the institutional planning language. With PDA there is no instrumental value in coveting someone else's resources as the means for survival, as is often the case now when "priorities" is the term used for suggesting vertical cuts for someone else. With PDA, it makes no difference that number 200 on my personal priority list is the first to become more like its future and less like its past, even if I am the President of the institution. This is a very different form of priorities. The achievement of better is "within" units, and is equally open to all units through participation and cooperation; priorities are not "between" units, nor achieved through the politics of power. Budget wars have been a tremendous waste of time, energy and money; they need to be replaced with an alternative that will work.

The Academic "Product"

The management challenge for higher education today is to have the courage to give effective voice to the requirements of our many customers. This is the first step; it is the one colleges and universities have been reluctant to take, and is why applying the TQM process to academic issues has been difficult. In higher education – unlike business – management to some degree serves, and to a large degree can be effective, only at the pleasure of the faculty. Most of the actual capacity for academic administrative roles is derived rather than vested in the position. Stated in a positive form, the faculty already have the considerable autonomy that TQM requires. The problem is, this autonomy also includes an unwillingness to give the requirements of the consumer an internal voice. The source of the necessary autonomy – academic freedom – is also the current source of the capacity for effective resistance. In the current climate of retrenchment, faculty feel threatened and act defensively. This is one of the reasons Deming has emphasized the need for freedom from fear for TQM to be effective (see Walton, 1986).

The non-specific and relativistic tone of an open-ended process may, at first, sound like weak leadership, but that is far from the case. TQM is not so much a passive relinquishing of a vision of the ends, as it is forcefully embracing the means to begin a process from which the end of greater sensitivity to customer requirements will emerge. Strong, central leadership is required to impose attention both on the requirements of the customers and on a process for giving those external demands internal legitimacy.

TQM requires genuine respect for those charged with the task. We need to dare to unleash the passion that can come only from genuinely engaging the academic community at each institution in the actual academic issues facing higher education (i.e., internal, local and specific). TQM takes strong leadership and a belief that greater attention to the needs of the consumer actually strengthens the true meaning of academic freedom – the power of innovation and change.

Although this chapter has not given an explicit definition of "the" standard of academic quality – such as either the great Western Works or the Great Modern Issues – it has directly addressed the problem of defining the academic product that TQM is to be applied to. This has been done, not by stating *what* they are as an absolute product – that would simply renew the national philosophical debates which are not getting us anywhere – but by providing a means whereby *all* at a given institution can participate in the production and ownership of a set of definitions and standards applicable to themselves. Although the crisis might be *in* higher education, it is *at* specific institutions where actual people have the capacity to act. If something is truly a process and is empowering, the correct answer cannot be decided in advance, by someone else, at some other place.

The example of TQM illustrates the creation of horizontal organizational involvement across the silos of institutional structures in a process of change in which those who are in the production line of teaching *and* learning (the relationship concept) assume immediate responsibility for the terms and conditions of their mutual engagement. It is a process that connects teachers and learners in a common enterprise, not through roles or positions of authority, but through a relationship fashioned from a common point. The result could never have been created or ordered from above by an administrator; only the situational conditions for engaging in the process can be ensured by management.

Women's Ways of Knowing

There is growing evidence that women approach problem solving and decision making differently than men (Belenky, et al., 1986). Men tend to maintain a critical distance with academic material in order to be objective and rational. Women tend to establish intimacy with the thinker and the material as the route to understanding (Clinchy, 1991). In moral reasoning, men tend to appeal to law and rules, but women will want to know the consequences – how the issue affects people – to make a judgment (Gilligan, 1982).

It is important to keep in mind that these are broad generalizations based on group differences between men and women. Like all personality dimensions there is a wide range of individual differences. Some men are more like the majority of women than they are to other men, and some women are more like the majority of men than like other women. Thus, it is not the contribution of individual women that is critical, because women come in many varieties as do men; but rather, the unique contribution of gender differences is to shift the proportional balance of the institutional culture toward greater emphasis on process, relationships and horizontal structure.

These differences find expression in many aspects of academic and community life. In teaching and learning, the greater incorporation of women's ways of knowing into the classroom will personalize the material, reduce the anonymity of large classes, enriching the learning experience and increasing the opportunity for men and women alike to be both connected and objective. In leadership, women view their role differently (Bensimon, 1991) and lead through greater use of consensus and sensitivity to relationships (Carnegie Foundation, 1990c). Feminism, the philosophical foundation of that yet-to-be-respected academic program of women's studies, may very well hold much of the wisdom necessary to meet the modern management challenge.

Conclusions

There are two roles required of academic leadership, that of managing change and of being an agent of change. These are often experienced as a paradox because the actions indicated for one are the contra-indications for the other. Effective leadership identifies the situations for which each is appropriate and avoids confusing the different ends that each serve. Both are called for at different times.

Periods of transition require new leadership qualities. Increasingly, as higher education undergoes the transformations necessary for a new era, becoming an agent of change will be more important than managing change (see Figure 13-1).

In the Post-Modern era the currency will become more one of adventure than one of discovery. The tasks ahead are not the creation of products as the criterion of leadership, but rather the introduction of processes that re-connect higher education with vital social, economic and political issues in order to reclaim the public trust (Bok, 1992). The criterion of success will be internal organizational change which – similar to successful industries – finds a way to break through the rule-bound bureaucratic legacy of the past era and move toward horizontal structures which are more adaptable and flexible (see e.g., Handy, 1989). These are learning opportunities which can be more quickly arranged to

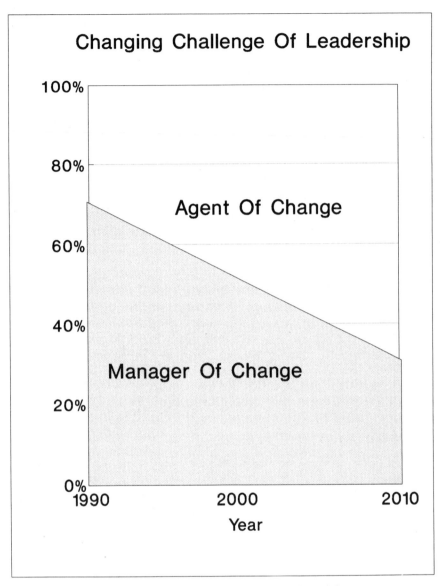

Figure 13-1: Academic Leadership

take advantage of the unique needs of specific people assembled in a particular place at a given time, often through alternative forms of instruction or material.

Such empowerment of a horizontal layer does not mean there are no standards. The only essential requirement is that each effort leave a trace and have the capacity to be self-correcting. A "learning" organization is one that incorporates effective feedback (such as PDA) into what it does, and by so doing makes change a continuous process (Senge, 1990). A college or university should be the ideal place to create a learning environment for the organization itself. Much more of what we do should be an experiment – an adventure.

Section Five
Prospect

This book began with the assertion that our beliefs and their implied definitions of the problems facing higher education had created a series of apparent dilemmas – such as choosing between internally-directed retrenchment or government intervention, between horizontal or vertical cuts, between unacceptable means for increasing revenue – either choice of which only compounded the problem the action was intended to solve. Such dilemmas can only be resolved by a process of re-definition which requires critically examining current beliefs in order to re-define the problems in a way which would create the academic, financial and management flexibility necessary to start a positive cycle of dynamism.

However, the choice for re-definition is never simple. The mind-set required to begin the process of re-definition is revolutionary in nature. Even asking the simple question of what the current issues of higher education would look like if viewed as *internal, local and specific* rather than *external, national and general*, disrupts the status quo in so fundamental a way as to insure resistance from those who, with their contrary views, will be swept aside.

The "revolutions" implied by re-definition can be as isolated as two people fundamentally altering their relationship, or as complex as a major re-ordering of world events, as in the agricultural and industrial revolutions. Between these two extremes of an interpersonal relationship and world events are such things as scientific revolutions, in which one branch of knowledge discards a theory and replaces it, along with its brokers and entrepreneurs, for a new one. This is called a paradigm shift, and it goes on every day, creating a major quake for one conceptually close to the centre, but often never felt by his or her geographic neighbor in the office next door. More than one revolution can be taking place at the same time, side by side, and the same person may be a major player in one and have no part in the other.

For some reason people shy away from the word "revolution," as if it was a negative rather than a positive happening in the grand sweep of human events, whereas humanistic accomplishments are the result of significant re-definitions. When I give workshops on change theory, I emphasize that from the psychology of the individual the modern personal challenge is not to be discarded. Unlike any previous time in human history, the capacity for personal survival is no longer the personal character and values that good parents instill in their children which will carry them through their life. This is now true because a person can no longer have a single belief system which will "see them out." Rather, human "evolution" is now an individual psychological process of personal survival which I have called "Psychological Darwinism." Although many may not know it, people of today are now players in an epochal drama and they can not escape participation. Re-definitions are intrusive and now increasingly individual, personal and psychological.

Two revolutions face higher education and therefore the people who give it a personal face. One revolution is going on in the world around us, and the other is our role and function in that world. The first is external and the second is internal. The individuals involved in higher education must either adapt or be discarded. Choices now facing higher education require a vision which gives a sense of coherence and self-direction to the field, focusing on the emergence of the New Era. The choice before those in higher education is either to raise a new vision and join in the quest for human survival, or remain on the sidelines as shapeless forms in the hands of fate.

This final section provides a glimpse of the total implications of the assumptions, beliefs, approaches, opportunities and challenges for change proposed in this monograph. In the single chapter of this section, I describe an exciting new university in the forefront of a transitional period of human history.

Chapter 14
Joining the Quest

Although most of the major current issues of higher education (e.g., cost-containment, incoherence in the curriculum, diversity and retrenchment) have been touched upon, the conceptual themes have been relatively few. The final task is to pull them together, not re-state them, into a faith that restores public confidence, defines a central role for higher education in the social and cultural context of the New Era, and energizes internally a sense of purpose that sustains adventure and excitement. Joining the quest for the New Era will involve discarding what is dysfunctional, embracing alternatives and raising a new vision.

The Myth of Intractability

The current problems of higher education are not difficult. There are many technical solutions to them, and most of these are well known and well understood. In addition, there is a huge store house of public good will, albeit taxed of recent, but not yet alienated; as a nation we believe in the power and value of knowledge for economic prosperity as well as for personal fulfillment and for equality of opportunity. This belief is shared by government, by university administrators, faculty, students, their parents, the general public and the business establishment. What more could be asked for?

It is true that there are important problems to be solved. There is a job to be done, a very important one; it starts with primary grades and ends with higher education. There are sufficient resources and the desire by all parties to accomplish the task. There can be no good excuse for failing to have done so over the decade of the 1990s.

The Weight of Retrospection

The good old days are gone, yet we hold on to them in so many ways. For too many years higher education has had to seek vitality without renewal. While some individual faculty have re-tooled and changed, most have not and cannot as a simple fact of human nature. Impatience and irreverence must come from those who are, not from those few who can understand, even correctly, its reasons and substance. The Career Alternatives Model and Position Description Analysis are two illustrative approaches for correcting a structural problem and nurturing the energy of dynamism.

Clearly, there are some truths to be claimed from the past; but not two-thirds worth of the total human investment capital. The excess is redundant and too heavy. We would not tolerate such an imbalance in our own retirement portfolio nor should we in our children's future fund. There are at least as many truths, probably many more, to be learned through actively reaching for the future.

The Adventure of Responsibility

The external focus, and the blaming of others has been bad for higher education. In relinquishing responsibility for the quality of local academic life, higher education has lost to external, amorphous and invisible forces what, in the end, people value most as human beings, a personal sense of responsibility.

Assuming individual responsibility for the vitality of their own academic life binds the individuals to each other; it makes each visible to the others. In the process each person becomes interdependent and therefore responsible to each other, and gains the most essential freedom, that of making choices that directly affect their own lives. The invisible life academics have developed, connected to the international community of scholars, but not to each other in any meaningful daily sense, has allowed them to escape responsibility and with it they have lost the freedom to control, direct and sustain the spiritual side of academic life (Lovett, 1993).

Constructive Alternativism

Re-examining beliefs about problems which seem intractable is so obvious and yet, because each individual must do so, so difficult once isolated from the collective support of community. The assumption which makes the choice to do so possible is the belief that similar to the creation of knowledge, it is failures and problems, not successes, that provide the opportunity for growth and change. The task is difficult because the problems caused by our beliefs are human ones, not technical ones, and their solutions are to be found by first looking to personality and social psychology (ourselves), not higher education.

Individual Psychology

I recently heard an advertisement on the radio for a telephone service called "We Care." The subscriber to the service can call anytime to complain about anything, no matter how trivial, e.g., "My feet hurt!", and the person on the other end of the phone line will "pretend that we really care." This example must surely exemplify the end of the Modern Era; it must be close to the last of the harmful items, like pills with red toxic die to make them pretty, mass produced, marketed and available for effortless consumption, but without commitment.

Post-Modern, New Era people are seeking new ways for finding meaning, for re-claiming *my* life, *my* time, and *my* space through participation which is inclusive. The information age makes this possible. While the world shrinks, and while each of us are connected in invisible economic and political ways with everyone else on the globe, we rightly feel overwhelmed. But, the same technology that has made that possible also gives us the power to have direct influence and control over much of our daily lives, such as the quality of campus life. Each professor need only be a computer keyboard stroke away from each of their students with far less effort and wasted time on both of their parts than regular office hours, the latter of which faculty are often required to keep, the former (the computer) not yet provided or required by many universities. If faculty and students are not to be isolated and alone, there must be specific, local and internal things which the parties do to be accountable to each other, or else all will be left with the alternative to a subscription to "We Care."

Isolation is not the choice people will make, given reasonable opportunities to rediscover responsibility for our campus life. Otherwise, without acceptable opportunities, pleas for greater responsibility by campus leadership is yet another contradiction of teaching one value while exemplifying the opposite.

Disestablishment

Why would "We Care" even have a chance? The answer is because higher education has helped to professionalize nearly everything, and this has been most destructive in the human services area. All of the professions have done this, and are taxing their members to campaign against a growing opposition to do so even more. For example, The American Psychology Association bought the magazine *Psychology Today* and for a time suffered an annual loss of two million dollars a year just to promote the business of professional psychology. The current trend is to expand accreditation to all applied branches of psychology.

Lawyers have done the same. Two people in a disagreement are increasingly the occasion for litigation rather than problem solving; and when mediation services are created they are professionalized to supposedly insure protection of rights. It is the professionals who become the principal financial beneficiaries of the arrangements.

We are constantly made to be dependent. If everything we bought had clear instructions and diagrams on how to take it apart, many of us could fix for ourselves what we now throw away or pay others to fix for us. But the best part is that people could share skills by fixing things for each other. Community is not hard to understand, nor are the mechanisms on which it is based.

Religion, science and education are powerful establishments. None of them can keep pace with the speed with which they are required to change to take care of us. The church, so heavy with tradition, is being faced with moral issues for which there is no immediate prospect of an acceptable answer, one after an other. Organized religion must relinquish its hold on proprietorship of what is right, and the individual must assume personal responsibility through the visibility that comes from community.

In the New Era there will not be learning independent of living or living independent of learning. The temporal delay of 25 years (grade 12, Bachelors,

MA, PhD, Post-Doc and then specialization) to begin living is already absurd, yet we are adding more criteria and delays to the process through accreditation and licensing of *professions* rather than of the possession of specific technical skills. Ninety percent of what professionals do uses only ten percent of their training. The role of higher education has been to provide academic sheltering of this process to keep the classrooms full and education as a growth industry. The justification has been that this is necessary because there is so much more to learn. It won't work. It is time to begin to reverse the process, to take down the barriers to participation and to freely disseminate knowledge. The goal is to put knowledge in the public, not commercial, sector.

The higher education establishment needs to give away knowledge, and with it, control over its use. Training comes in small functional packages which invites participation, first through the capacity for self-diagnosis about the nature of the problem, and second for greater choice over the kind of intervention that is appropriate – starting with self-help and progressing through the range of professional services.

What is the Age of Knowledge and the Information Age about if it is not CD ROM at every person's finger tips? Colleges and Universities need to get out of the business of facilitating (as an Industry and Establishment) mass ignorance and into the business of mass knowledge. The institutional winners of academic competition will not be determined through another decade of registration wars, but through the sharing of knowledge and information in immediately usable ways. Training is the gateway to education.

The Energy of Adventure

Once we have let the phrase, "this is a New Era," cross our lips in a meaningful way, the current problems fade into the exciting challenges of new opportunities and in the pursuit of adventures. To say and believe that this is the end of the Modern Era, rightly or wrongly, is to commit ourselves, our institutions and our students to an academic star trek into the future, against the residual dying values of the church, professionals and other modern establishments; this is what academic freedom is about. It is not freedom for reinstating the past and holding off the future, of that we can be definite.

The power of this position is the uncertainty it implies, which is what empowers a quest. By definition we cannot know the answer; we are simply at work on New Era problems. What a relief to be free from quarrelling over what is right! There is no product. We can listen to Bloom and Hirsch, and simply say "that is a silly discussion," and get on with the process of an adventure.

Our route is through what Alan Wicker (1989) has called "substantive theorizing." The New Era takes an immediate problem or issue as its focus, and next asks what needs to be known or learned (a methodological step) to understand it better? It deals first with the definition and explores the ingredients that may be helpful for re-definition. The final step is to ask, with this new information in hand, is there a better or more useful way to think? Re-definition (i.e., the concepts, theories, philosophies, in short what we think and believe) emerges as the final outcome of a process; what is being done or attempted comes first.

The New Era reverses the process of old science. We were taught to think deductively: To first have a concept, next to decide how to evaluate it, and then look for a manifestation. This is much too slow and awkward. Like picnics, life and knowledge are now participatory activities. The temporal pace of change is now too fast to first be educated in order to participate; we must now participate in order to become educated. The product that we say that we teach in our curriculum, what *should* be known, cannot be known in advance; there cannot be a curriculum of critical thoughts, only of substantive issues (unsolved problems) requiring critical thinking. Thus, the term "substantive theorizing" as the basis of New Era learning.

The "yes but" response is that students need to know how to write, count and think; therefore, we must first teach these basic skills. But, why can't they do that now? Because we have stretched the delay between learning and economic participation for periods of up to 25 years duration and growing, against all common sense, and in the process separated learning from living. The "therefore" that follows from the re-definition is to start the process of reversing the temporal delay and connecting learning and living. That is the quest.

Raising a New Vision

There is more than one way to learn the lesson of Don Quixote; it does not need to be by reading and discussing the work. The simple point that by creating and acting on an ideal, others will come to believe it, can be learned best by direct experience. The important lessons are perhaps best taught by behaviors and actions, including the lesson that the accomplishment of the impossible is in the belief and commitment to the quest. What better model for an academic adventure than the part of Don Quixote himself.

The Future is Now

The twenty-something generation is not deficient, much as our beliefs would have us think; the problem, for us, is that the alternative that **we** have failed them is unthinkable.

Each new era gains its energy from optimism. There was no reason, in theory, why the agricultural and industrial revolutions could not have eliminated the underclass. There is now enough wheat to feed the world's population; we simply do not do so for economic and political reasons.

Population growth and AIDS threaten the world, yet the Pope is against condoms. We say we want to teach values, but our society does not demand ethics in business or politics; we say we want to teach critical thinking, but don't expect critical thinking from presidential candidates and political leaders. We have failed as educators, and it is more and more evident that we are failing. Stated in the positive: it is time for something new. It is not success which is the occasion for humanistic accomplishment, it is the re-definitions which emerge from failure.

We are reduced to indecision by the twin conditions of depression and threat. Depression feeds inaction and passiveness (it is out of our control, up to "them" to save "us"), and threat feeds coercive, defensive, anti-change attitudes found in the search for certainty (the product of wisdom given out by the Pope, Bloom and those who claim to know what is best). Thus, we need the dual therapies of hope and adventure. The New Era, no less than those before, needs its promise and possibilities. The best part of the New Era is that you do not have to believe in something definite, you just have to believe.

Those of us who form the old guard had our dual quests of social justice through equality of access to education and to be first in science and technology. We wrote ourselves into a script and played it well, or not, as only history will judge. Because it was the end of an era we could be definite, efficient and above all else outcome directed; it is now time to be truly outrageous.

Outrageous U

I knew a woman assistant professor who started a consumer affairs class. She had her students research any issue they wished, e.g., the amount of needless toxins consumed each year, such as the red dye in the pretty pill. Soon she had enough material to do a weekly radio program. Then enough to start a hot-line staffed at set hours by the students, to answer questions if the information was in the file, or if not to add to the list of potential topics. The class grew in popularity; the more that came, the bigger and better the service got, which attracted more and more help. This is called dynamism; it is the opposite of the vicious circle of retrenchment.

This class connected learning and living; reading, writing and counting took care of themselves. A research piece needs to be well written; enter the writing lab part of the course, a time set aside when students read and responded to each other's work: Was it clear? Could it be said better? How? And, of course, the students sought help from writing experts, setting the stage for including rhetoric and for the same course to be two, not just one activity. Students learn by doing. The material soon got too big for a paper file; enter computers, and now three knowledge bases. The scope grew too large for one professor; enter a biologist committed to the environment who now could claim a legitimate, immediate and practical role for her academic passion.

Some, even among those on the sidelines, could imagine an integrated freshman year program. What excitement. But, in keeping with the philosophy of this book, it would have to be *a* program, not *the* program. There could be others; the question would *not* be which *one* is correct, but is this one acceptable, *too*.

But alas, of course, she was not a promotable academic. She did not publish research in peer evaluated journals and did not contribute to original scholarly knowledge; she simply collected low level information and gave it away. She is now a real estate salesperson, and is doing very well. She built up quite a following of people who know her name and respect and trust her. And, the university, now rid of its troublesome embarrassment, could get back to disciplined-based basics, the teaching of which they are so proud, as the way to prepare students for life.

At a local high school the principal started a day care in the school for the children of unwed teenage mothers, so they would not have to drop out of school. The daily care was the responsibility of the students in child development, home economics and health classes, with what they were to learn in the class connected with the day care – a learning laboratory, e.g., playing formal cognitive development games with the children to actually see the concepts.

The public opposition was massive: The program would encourage promiscuity! It was reinforcing illegitimacy! In fact, it kept girls in school, facilitating their future participation, and it connected learning and life for lots of students; and, I suspect, encouraged thoughtful awareness and spontaneous discussion about safe and sensible sex for many of the care-giving students who either were, or soon would be sexually active, the day care notwithstanding. This rich learning experience was immediately available simply by not hiding teenage pregnancy and its consequences. The concept is not very complicated or difficult; however, the courage and capacity to do it, and not to back down, was.

The list of possible ways to be outrageous could go on and on. I have already described how a community-base independent volunteer support service for victims of sexual assault grew out of one of my psychology classes. I have had community members, traditional students and policemen, both white and black, all enroled in a common course working on police-minority issues. I know of a department of psychology that once owned a tractor; it was used to turn vacant lots in the poor areas of the city into community vegetable gardens. Social interaction, communication, marketing all merged into a unified activity that cut across discipline, racial and university/community lines. Knowledge was given away, albeit not organized into discipline specific packages. The business officer, however, had a hard time seeing the tractor as no different than the photocopier – just another piece of knowledge-making apparatus, all part of the tools of the academic trade.

The examples I am using are not truly outrageous. In fact the only outrageous aspects of the examples are that they are seldom experienced by students, and when they are, they are regarded by many academics as not legitimate education. Even "service learning" is controversial to some and has been slow to develop despite the sound conceptual foundation provided long ago by Boyer & Hechinger (1981) and Newman (1985). The point is, we should make learning even more instrumental than we do, not just tacking it on to the college experience as a voluntary activity, as if life and experience are separate and contiguous, rather than simultaneous and overlapping.

Nothing else in life is linear and successive, why should we expect education for life to be any less so.

Academic Freedom

We have not for years taken the issue of academic freedom to the limit in the sense conveyed by a statement attributed to Einstein: "It gives me great pleasure indeed to see the stubbornness of an incorrigible nonconformist warmly acclaimed." The need has never been greater and the concept has never been weaker. Its most recent test, to challenge mandatory retirement, only helps to entrench the stats quo. Rather, academic freedom is becoming the freedom to be an academic. I am embarrassed to be part of an Establishment which has allowed such a fundamental concept to fall into such archaic status through disuse.

The task at hand is to start a revolution from within before solutions are imposed from without which will be based on a very different value system than what we within higher education have as our legacy, and still regard as timeless. In repressive societies, academics, journalists and the clergy are seen by authorities as a danger. The power of reflection and criticism is the enduring quest that binds our past with our future. We are about to lose what we should value most – the capacity to be agents of fundamental change – unless we lead and participate in, rather than resist, a challenge that is world-wide in its scope. We must join in the battle of human existence marked by the end of the Modern Era.

Stated in this way the emphasis is shifted from what are *the* correct definitions and structures (a product), to how to re-define and re-structure (a process). The first is substantive, while the second is social and psychological in nature.

What an Exciting Time to be Alive

That phrase was a theme of the popular book *Megatrends* (Naisbitt, 1982) a decade ago. It is an attitude that should characterize the university, but it does not. Who among us would choose, above all else, the university for its adventure and excitement?

Community and responsibility are achieved though participation. This fact is already well understood by our community colleges. The Carnegie Foundation (1990) noted that it was at community colleges where the students described the faculty as "truly caring," and spoke with gratitude about their classroom associations. Most important, we know that community and responsibility are the necessary conditions for a coherent sense of self-direction and values.

Although efforts to claim what will be may still be somewhat drawn from the past – an appropriate role of the elder – they will be largely achieved by reaching for an outrageous future. Where better than from within the walls of academia, where irreverence and impatience can be valued and where the mechanisms exist for them to be effectively defended if need be, and where, for students, there is a brief interlude from the normal constraints of survival to give them expression.

An Open Invitation

We do not have to fight with each other. The paradox of tradition and change can be a healthy tension; it is only destructive when we feel we must choose the unacceptable alternative of a continuation of present problems as a protection from the threat of the unknown.

There is no solution to be found by searching for a leader who has the vision of the "truth" about what we must achieve. The content must be open-ended. The substance of the future will take care of itself by making change a social and psychological possibility. The failure to look first to ourselves, and the conditions which give us the capacity to be bold, is to condemn ourselves to the sidelines.

We only need to create a small amount of space to give ourselves the luxury of choice, which I have called financial flexibility. We need only to dedicate this resource to begin an academic renewal process of creating the future, not recovering the past. We need only to nurture the process of dynamism to gain hope, energy and direction.

So cast, each of us within academe has the power and responsibility to control our own destiny through what we choose to believe. The issue is one of choice, and the "do nothing" alternative is, in fact, the choice of the status quo over some alternative. The identification of the choices before higher education are straightforward through the belief templates of this monograph.

Change or be Changed

The 1990s can be the period when it took slightly less than a decade to reduce the temporal gap between learning and living and for training to become the means for education, led from within by our colleges and universities in a new academic revolution. Or, the 1990s can be the period when it took slightly more than a decade to reduce the temporal gap between learning and living and for training to become the means for education, led from outside higher education by external interventions which levels much of the existing four-year higher education system to become reluctantly more like community colleges and increasingly relies on private information sources as the major brokers of common knowledge, with most campuses overbuilt and under-used. Simply put, we will let universities as we know them die, next in line behind the railroad and the post office.

Retrenchment or Dynamism

Either serious scholarship and research of uncommon knowledge (i.e., the very expensive high technology of modern science) will be broken off from living and learning and concentrated in a few elite research institutions, and common education will be left to the bitter losers, to thriving community colleges, and to the growing number of proprietary schools which will meet the market demand more cheaply and competitively. With this choice the PhD and the faculty shortage will be avoided, and individuals dedicated to teaching can be hired for their specialized knowledge, often as a supplement to their full-time line of work, bridging the campus gap between business and community more easily and effectively than the cooperation and alliances as we now know them (Handy, 1989).

Or, the new academic revolution can be joined from within, and in this decade the collective body of higher education will re-discover the responsibilities of community and will join with its students in the celebration of a New Era. The very brightest will find their way into the PhD programs, often as a result of their "training" from whomever will provide it, but through the joyous route of a shared adventure, not the arduous task of long-term compliance and good citizenship.

Post-Modern

The belief in the essential roles of reflection and criticism – the obligation and responsibility to be an agent of change – in the quest of the "Age of Knowledge" may be no less of an illusion than were our beliefs in the virtues of the joint quests of the 1960s. But, now as then, it is our beliefs which will or will not allow us to join in the celebration of a New Era.

References

AAHE Task Force on Professional Growth. (1983). *Vitality without mobility: The faculty opportunities audit.* Washington, D.C.: American Association for Higher Education.

Alexander, L. (1986). *Time for results: The governors' 1919 report on education.* Washington, D.C.: National Governors' Association. The reports on "College Quality" were reprinted along with selected other material in the *Chronicle of Higher Education, 33* (1, Sept. 3), 78-90.

Altbach, P.G. & Lewis, L.S. (1992). The professor's lot. *Change, 24* (6, Nov/Dec), 8-9.

Anisef, P. & Okihiro, N. (1982). *Losers and winners: The pursuit of equality and social justice in higher education.* Toronto, Canada: Butterworths.

Association of Commonwealth Universities. (1985). The Jarratt report: *A.C.U. Bulletin of Current Documentation, 69* (June), 2-6.

Astin, A.W. (1987). Competition or cooperation? Teaching teamwork as a basic skill. *Change, 19* (5, Sept./Oct.), 12-19.

Astin, A.W. (1993). This year's college freshman: A statistical profile. *Chronicle of Higher Education, 39* (19, Jan. 13), 30-31.

Astin, A.W., Green, K.C. & Korn, W.S. (1987). *The American freshman: Twenty year trends.* Los Angeles: Higher Education Research Institute, University of California Los Angeles.

Astin, A.W., Korn, W.S. & Dey, E.L. (1991). *The American college teacher.* Los Angeles: Higher Education Research Institute, University of California Los Angeles.

Bailey, A.L. (1987). Using literature to analyze moral issues: Brandeis U. program helps professionals confront dilemmas in their careers. *Chronicle of Higher Education, 33* (20), 3.

Barber, B.R. (1992). *An aristocracy of everyone: The politics of education and the future of America.* New York: Ballantine Books.

Barnett, R. (1990). *The idea of higher education.* Bristol, PA: Open University Press.

Belenky, M.F., Clinchy, B.M., Goldberger, N.G. & Tarule, J.M. (1986). *Women's ways of knowing: The development of self, voice, and mind.* New York: Basic Books.

Bell, D. (1987). *And we are not saved: The elusive quest for racial justice.* New York: Basic Books.

Bensimon, E.M. (1991). A feminist reinterpretation of president's definitions of leadership. *Peabody Journal of Education, 68* (4), In Press.

Bercuson, D., Bothwell, R. & Granatstein, J.L. (1984). *The great brain robbery.* Toronto: McCelland & Stewart.

Bernstein, A. (1990). Students on campus: Sex, race, and diversity tapes. *Change, 22* (2, Mar./April), 18-23.

Bloom, A. (1987). *The closing of the American mind.* New York: Simon & Schuster.

Blum, D.E. (1990a). Vatican bars theologians from public dissent on official teachings of the Catholic Church. *Chronicle of Higher Education, 36* (42, July 5), 1, 15.

Blum, D.E. (1990b). The Vatican releases long-awaited document that explains its authority over Catholic institutions around the world. *Chronicle of Higher Education, 37* (5, Oct. 3), 19 & 22.

Blum, D.E. (1990c). Temple U. copes with aftermath of its bitter strike: Anger and breakdown of campus relationships. *Chronicle of Higher Education, 37* (10, Nov.7), 13-15.

Blum, D.E. (1991). Environment still hostile to women in academe new evidence indicates. *Chronicle of Higher Education, 38* (7, Oct. 9), 1, 20.

Blumenstyk, G. (1991). Bleak economic outlook forces states to seek more revenue from their public-college students. *Chronicle of Higher Education, 37* (25, March 6), 1, 26.

Blumenstyk, G. & Cage, M.C. (1991). Public colleges expect financial hardship in 1991 as budget crises imperil state appropriations. *Chronicle of Higher Education, 37* (17, Jan. 9), 1, 20-31.

Bok, D. (1986). *Higher learning.* Cambridge, MA: Harvard University Press.

Bok, D. (1990). *Universities and the future of America.* Durham, NC: Duke University Press.

Bok, D. (1992). Reclaiming the public trust. *Change, 24* (4, July/Aug.), 12-19.

Botstein, L. (1990). The college presidency: 1970-1990. *Change, 22* (2, Mar./April), 34-40.

Bowen, H.R. (1983). The art of retrenchment. *Academe, 69* (1), 21-24.

Bowen, H.R. & Schuster, J.H. (1986). *American professors: A national resource imperiled.* New York: Oxford University Press.

Boyer, E.L. (1987). *College: The undergraduate experience in America.* New York: Harper & Row.

Boyer, E.L. (1990). *Scholarship reconsidered: Priorities of the professoriate.* Lawrenceville, NJ: Princeton University Press.

Boyer, E.L. & Hechinger, F.M. (1981). *Higher learning in the nation's service.* Washington: Carnegie Foundation.

Burbules, N.C. & Densmore, K. (1991). The limits of making teaching a profession. *Education Policy, 5,* 44-63.

Cage, M.C. (1991). 30 States cut higher-education budgets by an average of 3.9% in fiscal 1990-91. *Chronicle of Higher Education, 37* (41, June 26), 1, 17.

Carnegie Council on Policy Studies in Higher Education. (1980). *Three thousand futures: The next twenty years for higher education.* San Francisco: Jossey-Bass.

Carnegie Foundation for the Advancement of Teaching. (1989). *The condition of the professoriate: Attitudes and trends.* Lawrenceville, NJ: Princeton University Press.

Carnegie Foundation for the Advancement of Teaching. (1990a). *Campus life: In search of community.* Lawrenceville, NJ: Princeton University Press.

Carnegie Foundation for the Advancement of Teaching. (1990b). Early faculty retirees: Who, why and with what impact? *Change, 22* (4, July/Aug.), 31-34.

Carnegie Foundation for the Advancement of Teaching. (1990c). Women faculty excel as campus citizens. *Change, 22* (5, Sept./Oct.), 39-43.

Carothers, R.L. (1992). Trippingly on the tongue: Translating quality for the academy. *AAHE Bulletin, 45* (3, Nov.), 6-10.

Chabotar, K. & Honan, J.P. (1990). Coping with retrenchment: Strategies and tactics. *Change, 22* (6, Nov./Dec.), 28-38.

Clinchy, B.M. (1991). Tales told out of school: Women's reflections on their undergraduate experience. *Teaching Excellence, 3* (4), 1-4.

Collison, M. (1988). Students at Ohio U flock to a course in which humor is a serious business, right down to the final examination. *Chronicle of Higher Education, 34* (35, May 11), 26-27.

Collison, M. (1990). Survey at Rutgers suggests that cheating may be on the rise at large universities. *Chronicle of Higher Education, 37* (8, Oct. 24), 31-32.

Collison, M. (1991a). More traditional-age students consider community colleges. *Chronicle of Higher Education, 37* (30, April 10), 1, 29-30.

Collison, M. (1991b). Increase in reports of sexual assaults strains campus disciplinary systems. *Chronicle of Higher Education, 37* (35, May 15), 29-30.

Collison, M. (1992). Colleges find aggressive recruiting pays off in larger freshman classes this fall. *Chronicle of Higher Education, 39* (11, Nov. 4), 27 & 29.

Cornesky, R., McCool, S., Byrnes, L. & Weber, R. (1992). *Implementing total quality management in higher education.* Madison, WI: Magna.

Cross, P. (1987). Teaching *for* learning. *AAHE Bulletin, 39* (8, April), 3-7.

Cross, P. (1988). In search of zippers. *AAHE Bulletin, 40* (10, June), 3-7.

Cross, P. (1990). Teachers as scholars. *AAHE Bulletin, 43* (4, Dec.), 3-5.

Cross, P. (1991). Reflections, predictions, and Paradigm shifts. *AAHE Bulletin, 43* (9, May), 9-12.

Deming, W.E. (1986). *Out of crisis.* Cambridge, MA: MIT Center for Advanced Engineering Study.

DeMott, B. (1990). The age at variance. *Change, 22* (2, Mar./April), 24-29.

Dill, B.T. & Dill, J.R. (1990). To be mature, tenured, and black: Reflections on 20 years of academic partnership. *Change, 22* (2, Mar./April), 30-33.

Dodge, S. (1990). Despite the crime, noise, and stress, most students at urban colleges relish the lessons of the city life. *Chronicle of Higher Education, 37* (13, Nov. 28), 35 & 37.

Dodge, S. (1991a). More college students choose academic majors that meet social and environmental concerns. *Chronicle of Higher Education, 37* (14, Dec. 5), 1, 31-32.

Dodge, S. (1991b). Average score on SAT verbal sections falls to all-time low; MAT score declines first time in more than ten years. *Chronicle of Higher Education, 38* (2, Sept. 4), 45 & 48.

Eble, K.E. & McKeachie, W.J. (1985). *Improving undergraduate education through faculty development.* San Francisco: Jossey-Bass.

Edgerton, R. (1987). The Springhill statement. *AAHE Bulletin, 40* (3, Nov.), 3-4.

Edgerton, R. (1988). Help wanted: "Education Presidents." *AAHE Bulletin, 41* (3, Nov.), 9-10.

Edgerton, R. (1989). Report from the President. *AAHE Bulletin, 41* (10), 14-17.

Edgerton, R. (1991). National standards are coming! *AAHE Bulletin, 44* (4, Dec.), 8-12.

Elmore, R.F. (1989). How we teach is what we teach. *AAHE Bulletin, 41* (8, April), 11-14.

Eurich, N.P. (1985). *Corporate classrooms: The learning business.* Lawrenceville, NJ: Princeton University Press.

Eurich, N.P. (1991). *The learning industry: Education for adult workers*. Lawrenceville, NJ: Princeton University Press.

Evangelauf, J. (1990a). Fees rise more slowly this year, but surpass inflation rate again. *Chronicle of Higher Education, 37* (4, Oct. 3), 1 & 36.

Evangelauf, J. (1990b). Report laments the 'disappearance' of the private liberal-arts college. *Chronicle of Higher Education, 37* (3, Sept. 19), 2.

Evangelauf, J. (1991). 1991 tuition increases expected to outpace inflation, but some private colleges will slow upward trend. *Chronicle of Higher Education, 37* (25, March 6), 1, 27.

Evangelauf, J. (1992a). Minority-group enrollments rose 10% from 1988 to 1990, reaching record levels. *Chronicle of Higher Education, 38* (20, Jan. 22), 33& 37.

Evangelauf, J. (1992b). Tuition at public colleges is up by 10% this year, College Board study finds. *Chronicle of Higher Education, 39* (9, Oct. 21), 36-43.

Faludi, S. (1991). *Backlash: The undeclared war against American women*. New York: Doubleday.

Fuchsberg, G. (1988). $20-billion needed to save crumbing campus buildings, a survey finds. *Chronicle of Higher Education, 34* (46, July 17), 13.

Gardner, C., Warner, T.R. & Biedenweg, R. (1990). Stanford and the railroad: Case studies of cost cutting. *Change, 22* (Nov./Dec.), 23-27.

Giddings, P.J. (1990). A legacy of the 60s: Education, race and reality. *Change, 22* (2, Mar./April), 10-17.

Gilligan, C. (1982). *In a different voice: Psychological theory and women's development*. Cambridge, MA: Harvard University Press.

Grassmuck, K. (1990a). Some research universities contemplate sweeping changes, ranging from management and tenure to teaching methods. *Chronicle of Higher Education, 37* (Sept. 12), 1, 29-31.

Grassmuck, K. (1990b). Colleges scrabble for money to reduce huge maintenance backlog, estimated to exceed $70-billion; new Federal help seen unlikely. *Chronicle of Higher Education, 37* (6, Oct. 10), 1 & 34.

Handy, C. (1989). *The age of unreason*. Boston, MA: Harvard Business School Press.

Halfond, J.A. (1991). Too many administrators: How it happened and how to respond. *AAHE Bulletin, 43* (7, March), 7-8.

Heller, S. (1990). Colleges becoming havens of 'political correctness,' some scholars say. *Chronicle of Higher Education, 37* (12, Nov. 21), 1 & 14.

Hirsch, E.D. (1987). *Cultural literacy*. Boston: Houghton Mifflin.

Illich, I. (1971). *Deschooling society*, 1st ed. New York: Harper & Row.

Illich, I. (1976). *Medical nemesis*. New York: Pantheon Books.

Iacocca, L. (1984). *Iacocca: An autobiography*. New York: Bantam.

Jacobson, R.L. (1985). New Carnegie data show faculty members uneasy about the state of academe and their own careers. *Chronicle of Higher Education, 31* (16, Dec. 18), 1, 24-28.

Jacobson, R.L. (1992). Colleges face new pressures to increase faculty productivity. *Chronicle of Higher Education, 38* (32, April 15), 1, 16-18.

Jaschik, S. (1990). State spending $40.8-billion on colleges this year; growth rate at a 30-year low. *Chronicle of Higher Education, 37* (8, Oct. 24), 1 & 26.

Jaschik, S. (1992). 1% decline in state support for colleges thought to be first 2-year drop ever. *Chronicle of Higher Education, 39* (9, Oct. 21), 21, 26-28.

Jencks, C. & Riesman, D. (1969). *The academic revolution*. Garden City, NY: Doubleday.

Kelly, G. (1955). *The psychology of personal constructs*. New York: Norton.

Kennedy, D. (1987). The letter: 37 Presidents write... *AAHE Bulletin, 40* (3, Nov.), 10-14.

Kolodny, A. (1991), Colleges must recognize students' cognitive styles and cultural backgrounds. *Chronicle of Higher Education, 37* (21, Feb. 6), 44.

Koestler, A. (1971). *The case of the midwife toad*. New York: Random House.

Koestler, A. (1973). *The call girls*. New York: Random House.

Kuhn, T.S. (1970). *The structure of scientific revolutions*, 2nd. ed. Chicago: University of Chicago Press.

Langfitt, T.W. (1990). The cost of higher education: Lessons from the health care industry. *Change, 22* (6), 8-15.

Leatherman, C. (1990). At Brandeis U., an intense debate over how to keep its traditional identity. *Chronicle of Higher Education, 37* (8, Oct. 24), 1 & 13.

Leatherman, C. (1991). From poetry to politics, professors tie their teachings to the Persian Gulf War. *Chronicle of Higher Education, 37* (21, Feb. 6), 1 & 16.

Leatherman, C. (1992). Isolation of pioneering feminist scholar stirs reappraisal of women's status in academe. *Chronicle of Higher Education, 39* (12, Nov. 11), 17-18.

Lennards, J. (1987). *The academic profession in Canada: Final report*. Ottawa: Social Sciences and Humanities Research Council.

Leslie, P.M. (1980). *Canadian universities: 1980 and beyond*. Ottawa: Association of Universities and Colleges of Canada.

Lewis, R.G. & Smith, D.H. (1994). *Total quality in higher education*. Delray Beach, FL: St. Lucie Press.

Lively, K. & Mercer, J. (1993). Little relief in sight. *Chronicle of Higher Education, 39* (18, Jan. 6), 29-38.

Lovett, C.M. (1993). To affect intimately the lives of people: American professors and their society. *Change, 25*, 26-37.

Magner, D.K. (1989). Blacks and whites on the campuses: Behind ugly racist incidents, student isolation and insensitivity. *Chronicle of Higher Education, 35* (33, April 26), 1, 28-31.

Magner, D.K. (1990a). Racial tensions continue to erupt on campuses despite efforts to promote cultural diversity. *Chronicle of Higher Education, 37* (38, June 6), 1, 29-30.

Magner, D.K. (1990b). 9 in 10 Americans say people can't afford college. *Chronicle of Higher Education, 37* (7, Oct. 17), 2.

Magner, D.K. (1990c). Amid the diversity, racial isolation remains at Berkeley. *Chronicle of Higher Education, 37* (11, Nov. 14), 37-39.

Mangan, K.S. (1989). Trinity's 'logical detectives' stalk Jack the Ripper: Would Socrates have approved? *Chronicle of Higher Education, 35* (45, July 19), 1, 25.

Mangan, K.S. (1990). Battle rages over plan to focus on race and gender in U. of Texas course. *Chronicle of Higher Education, 37* (12, Nov. 21), 15.

Mangan, K.S. (1991). More colleges resort to faculty and staff layoffs in response to sluggish U. S. economy. *Chronicle of Higher Education, 38* (12, Nov. 13), 37-38.

Marchese, T. (1991). TQM reaches the academy. *AAHE Bulletin, 44* (3, Nov.), 10-13, 18.

Marchese, T. (1992). AAHE and TQM. *AAHE Bulletin, 45* (3, Nov.), 11.

Menges, R.J. & Svinicki, M.D. (1991). *College teaching: From theory to practice.* New Directions for Teaching and Learning, No. 45. San Francisco: Jossey-Bass.

Miller, M.K. (1983). Health systems vs. sickness systems: Implications for the physical well-being of Americans, pp 59-77. In R.F. Morgan (ed.), *The iatrogenics handbook.* Toronto, Canada: IPI Publishing.

Moffatt, M. (1990). *Undergraduate cheating.* New Brunswick, NJ: Department of Anthropology, Rutgers University.

Monaghan, P. (1990). Mills College faces a demographic and educational dilemma: Can it admit men but remain a leader in women's education? *Chronicle of Higher Education, 36* (29, April 4), 37.

Mooney, C.J. (1989). Professors are upbeat about profession but uneasy about student standards. *Chronicle of Higher Education, 36* (10, Nov. 13), 1, 18-21.

Mooney, C.J. (1990). Academic group fighting the 'politically correct left' gains momentum. *Chronicle of Higher Education, 37* (15, Dec. 12), 1, 13 & 16.

Mooney, C.J. (1992). Critics within and without academe assail professors at research universities. *Chronicle of Higher Education, 39* (10, Oct. 28), 17-19.

Morgan, R.F., Ed. (1983). *The iatrogenics handbook.* Toronto, Canada: IPI Publishers.

Naisbitt, J. (1982). *Megatrends.* New York: Warner Books.

Naisbitt, J. & Aburdene, P. (1990). *Megatrends 2000.* New York: William Marrow & Co.

National Commission on Excellence in Education. (1983). *A nation at risk.* Washington, DC: U.S.G.P.O., 65 pp.

Newman, F. (1985). *Higher education and the American resurgence.* Lawrenceville, NJ: Princeton University Press.

Nicklin, J. & Blumenstyk, G. (1993). Number of non-teaching staff members continues to grow in higher education. *Chronicle of Higher Education, 39* (18, Jan. 6), 43 & 46.

O'Keefe, M. (1987). A new look at college costs: Where does the money really go? *Change, 19* (6, Nov./Dec.), 12-39.

O'Neill, P. (1988). Academic reform as community intervention. *Canadian Psychology, 29,* 362-365.

O'Neill, P. & Trickett, E.J. (1982). *Community consultation.* San Francisco: Jossey-Bass.

Ornstein, R. & Ehrlich, P. (1989). *New world new mind.* New York: Double Day.

Palmer, P.L. (1987). Community, conflict, and ways of knowing: Ways to deepen our education agenda. *Change, 19* (5, Sept./Oct.), 20-25.

Panabaker, J.H. (1988). Government incentives and business connections: Faustian pacts? In A.L. Darling & A.D. Gregor (eds.) *Higher education: A changing scene.* Winnipeg, MB: Office of Higher Education Management, University of Manitoba.

Pascarell, E.T. & Terenzini, P.J. (1991). *How college affects students.* San Francisco: Jossey-Bass.

Patton, V.C. (1983). Voluntary alternatives to forced termination. *Academe, 69* (No.1), 1-8.

Rappaport, J. (1977). *Community psychology: Values, research and action.* New York: Holt, Rinehart and Winston.

Rappaport, J. (1981). In praise of paradox: A social policy of empowerment over prevention. *American Journal of Community Psychology, 9*, 1-25.

Rau, W. & Baker, P.J. (1989). The organized contradictions of academe: Barriers facing the next academic revolution. *Teaching Sociology, 17*, 161-175.

Renner, K.E. (1986a). Career alternatives: A model for calculating financial costs and making policy decisions. *Research in Higher Education, 25*, 42-54.

Renner, K.E. (1986b). Career alternatives: Providing a cafeteria of choices through career alternative dollars. *Research in Higher Education, 25*, 227-244.

Renner, K.E. (1986c). Tenure, retirement, and the year 2000: The issue of flexibility and dollars. *Research in Higher Education, 25*, 307-315.

Renner, K.E. (1987). Academic decision making: Faculty appointment and re-appointments. *Research in Higher Education, 26*, 363-372.

Renner, K.E. (1988a). Replacing retrenchment with dynamism through a program of career alternatives. *Canadian Psychology, 29*, 342-354.

Renner, K.E. (1988b), Raising a new vision of higher education. *Canadian Psychology, 29*, 365-368.

Renner, K.E. (1991). A survey tool, retrenchment blues, and a career alternatives program. *Canadian Journal of Higher Education, 21*, In Press.

Renner, K.E. (1992). Attitudes and demographics of higher education. Paper presented to the Canadian Society for the Study of Higher Education, Charlottetown, PEI, June 9, 1992.

Renner, K.E. (1993). On race and gender in higher education: Illusions of change. *Educational Record, 74* (No. 4, Fall), 44-48.

Renner, K.E. & Gierach, D. (1975). An approach to the problem of identifying policemen who use force excessively. *Journal of Police Science and Administration, 3*, 377-383.

Renner, K.E. & Keith, A. (1985). The establishment of a crisis intervention service for victims of sexual assault. *Canadian Journal of Community Mental Health, 4*, 113-123.

Renner, K.E. & Mwenifumbo, L. (1995). Renewal, costs and university faculty demographics. *Educational Quarterly Review, 2* (3), In Press.

Renner, K.E., & Skibbens, R. (1990). Position description analysis: A method for describing academic roles and functions. *Canadian Journal of Higher Education, 20*, 43-56.

Rosenzweig, R.M. (1989). Thatcherism in higher education: California, here she comes. *Change, 21* (Sept./Oct.), 40-41.

Ryan, W. (1971). *Blaming the victim*. New York: Vintage Books.

Sanday, P.R. (1990). *Fraternity gang rape: Sex, brotherhood, and privilege on campus*. New York: New York University Press.

Sarason, S.B. (1972). *The creation of settings and the future societies*. San Francisco: Jossey-Bass.

Sarason, S.B. (1978). The nature of social problem solving in social action. *American Psychologist, 33*, 370-380.

Seidman, E. & Rappaport, J., Eds. (1986). *Redefining social problems*. New York: Plenum Press.

Senge, P. (1990). *The fifth discipline*. New York: Doubleday.

Shalala, D. (1989). On changing the academic culture from the inside. *Change, 21* (1, Jan./Feb.), 20-29.

Shattock, M. (1989). Thatcherism and British higher education: Universities and the enterprise culture. *Change, 21* (5, Sept./Oct.), 30-39.

Shea, C. (1992). Protests centering on racial issues erupt on many campuses this fall. *Chronicle of Higher Education, 39* (14, Nov. 25), 23-24.

Sherwin, S. & Renner, K.E. (1979). Respect for persons in a study of the use of force by police officers. *Clinical Research, 27*, 19-22.

Shulman. L.S. (1987). Learning to teach. *AAHE Bulletin, 40* (3, Nov.), 5-9.

Shulman, L.S. (1989). Toward a pedagogy of substance. *AAHE Bulletin, 41* (10, June), 8-13.

Simpson, W.A. (1985). Retrenchment in British universities: Lessons learned. *Canadian Journal of Higher Education, 15*, 73-91.

Smith, P. (1989). Leadership, vision and good faith. *CAUT Bulletin, 36* (Dec.), 3 & 16.

Sykes, C. (1989). *Prof-scam: Professors and the demise of higher education.* Washington, DC: Regnery Gateway.

Symons, T.H.B. & Page, J.E. (1984). *Some questions of balance: Human resources, higher education and Canadian studies.* Ottawa, ON: Association of Universities and Colleges of Canada.

Task Force on Teaching As a Profession. (1986). *A nation prepared: Teachers for the 21st century.* New York: Carnegie Corporation, Carnegie Forum on Education and the Economy.

Taylor-Russell, A. (1986). A history of UK's first-ever national strike. *CAUT Bulletin, 33* (Sept.), 25.

Tierney, W.G. (1988). Organizational culture in higher education. *Journal of Higher Education, 59*, 2-21.

Tierney, W.G. (1991). Academic work and institutional culture: Constructing knowledge, *The Review of Higher Education, 14*, 199-216.

Timmons, B. (1989). Career progress and satisfaction among Canadian academics. *The Alberta Journal of Educational Research, 35*, 325-336.

Wagner, J. (1987). Teaching and research as student responsibilities: Integrating community and academic work. *Change, 19* (5, Sept./Oct.), 26-35.

Wallace, C. (1990). Colleges should develop new ways to meet the training needs of business. *Chronicle of Higher Education, 37* (16, Dec. 19), 36.

Walsh, R. (1984). *Staying Alive: The Psychology of Human Survival.* Boston: New Science Library.

Walton, M. (1986). *The Deming Management Method.* New York: Putnam.

Watkins, B.T. (1986). Stable and stagnant senior professors said to resist changes in their lives. *Chronicle of Higher Education, 32* (8, April 23), 21 & 28.

Watkins, B.T. (1989). Boston University may soon get the opportunity it wants: to run – and reform – a city's schools. *Chronicle of Higher Education, 35* (31, April 12), 1, 16-17.

Watkins, B.T. (1990a). Boston U. and Chelsea are optimistic, but wary, as they start 2nd year of school reform project. *Chronicle of Higher Education, 37* (6, Oct. 10), 14 & 17.

Watkins, B.T. (1990b). From music classes in early grades to literacy projects for adults, B. U. hopes Chelsea experiments will be model for urban schools. *Chronicle of Higher Education, 37* (6, Oct. 10), 14 & 18.

Watkins, B.T. (1991). Issues of racial and social diversity are the centerpiece of revamped freshman writing course at U. of Mass. *Chronicle of Higher Education, 37* (16, Dec. 19), 13-14.

Weimer, M. (1990). The scholarship of teaching. *The Journal of Professional Studies, 13* (3), 4-20.

Werth, B. (1988). Why is college so expensive? *Change, 20* (2, Mar./April), 13-25.

Whipple, W.R. (1987). Collaborative learning: Recognizing it when we see it. *AAHE Bulletin, 40* (2), 3-6.

Whittington, M.C. (1992). TQM at Penn: A report on first experiences. An interview with Marna C. Whittington by Ted Marchese. *AAHE Bulletin, 45* (3, Nov.), 3-5, 14.

Wicker, A. (1989). Substantive theorizing. *American Journal of Community Psychology, 17*, 531-547.

Wilbur, F.P. & Lambert, L.M. (1990). *Linking America's schools and colleges: Guide to partnership and national directory*. Washington, DC: American Association for Higher Education.

Wilson, R. (1989). Colleges' anti-harassment policies bring controversy over free-speech issues. *Chronicle of Higher Education, 36* (5, Oct. 4), 38-39.

Wilson, R. (1990a). College recruiting gimmicks get more lavish as competition for new freshmen heats up. *Chronicle of Higher Education, 36* (25, Mar. 7), 1 & 34.

Wilson, R. (1990b). As competition for students increases admissions officers face dismissal if they don't win and keep on winning. *Chronicle of Higher Education, 37* (9, Oct. 31), 1 & 36.

Wilson, R. (1991). Undergraduates at large universities found to be increasingly dissatisfied. *Chronicle of Higher Education, 37* (17, Jan. 19), 1, 37-38.

Yurchesyn, K., Keith, A. & Renner, K.E. (1992). Contrasting perspectives on the nature of sexual assault provided by a service for sexual assault victims and by the law courts. *Canadian Journal of Behavioural Science, 24*, 71-85.

Zemsky, R. & Massy, W.E. (1990). Cost-containment: Committing to a new economic reality. *Change, 22* (6, Nov./Dec.), 16-22.

Zwerling, L.S. (1988). The Miami-Dade Story. *Change, 20* (1, Jan./Feb.), 10-23.

Index